African Americans
in the South

African Americans in the South

*Issues of Race,
Class, and Gender*

Hans A. Baer and
Yvonne Jones, Editors

Southern Anthropological Society Proceedings, No. 25
Mary W. Helms, Series Editor

The University of Georgia Press
Athens and London

Southern Anthropological Society

Founded 1966

© 1992 by the Southern Anthropological Society
Published by the University of Georgia Press
Athens, Georgia 30602
All rights reserved

Set in Times Roman
The paper in this book meets the guidelines for
permanence and durability of the Committee on
Production Guidelines for Book Longevity of the
Council on Library Resources.

Printed in the United States of America

96   95   94   93   92   C   5   4   3   2   1

Library of Congress Cataloging in Publication Data

African Americans in the South : issues of race, class, and gender /
Hans A. Baer and Yvonne Jones, editors.
    p.   cm. — (Southern Anthropological Society proceedings ; no. 25)
    Includes bibliographical references (p.   ).
    ISBN 0-8203-1376-9 (alk. paper. — ISBN 0-8203-1377-7 (pbk. : alk.
paper)
    1. Afro-Americans—Southern States—Social conditions.
2. Southern States—Social conditions.   3. Southern States—Race
relations.   I. Baer, Hans A., 1944–   II. Jones, Yvonne.
III. Series.
GN2.S9243   no. 25
[E185.92]
305.896′073075—dc20   91-17728
                                           CIP

British Library Cataloging in Publication Data available

Contents

Foreword: The South in US and US in the South

Johnnetta Cole

A recent *Time* magazine article stated that by the not-so-distant year 2020, "a date no further than John F. Kennedy's election is in the past," the "white" population of the United States will have ceased increasing, while the number of "Hispanics and nonwhites" will have more than doubled to almost 115 million. By 2056 the "average" U.S. resident, as defined by census statistics, will trace his or her descent from Africa, Asia, the Hispanic world, the Pacific Islands, Arabia—almost anywhere but white Europe (9 April 1990, 28). These statistics may startle, even frighten many Americans. To those of us who work in ethnically diverse communities in the United States, including the South, these numbers simply confirm what we already know: America is numerically as well as culturally an incredibly diverse nation. This is a fact we anthropologists of American culture have known for a long time. And certainly some anthropologists have argued that this ethnic and cultural diversity is *increasing* in complexity, not dissipating or withering away or even melting into one pot dominated by a single white European American ingredient. Indeed, when we think of the indigenous people of the United States we have to ask if America was ever a monolithic culture.

Then, what does this have to do with those of us (anthropologists and educators) who already know these statistics; those of us who take a certain pride in our knowledge, acceptance, and even appreciation of cultural and ethnic diversity? After all, don't we all teach about the *richness* of diversity (as opposed to its imminent "threat" to some xenophobic fantasy of a monolithic America)? Certainly we anthropologists have discussed, written about, even lectured on the political and economic ramifications of racial and cultural diversity. Many of us have even organized inside and outside of the academy around these issues.

As anthropologists of the South and as southern anthropologists, we teach our students about the richness of this region, its racist-ridden past, out of which has sprung a "New South"—more conscious of that racism and, therefore, in a better position to eradicate it. We applaude the recent electoral achievements of African Americans in the South as well as the reality that over one half of all elected African American officials in the United States are in the South.

But while we look to the New South with hope, we anthropologists must critically analyze and even take a stand opposing the vandalism against black churches in Spartanburg, South Carolina; the election of David Duke, former grand wizard of the Ku Klux Klan; and the recent racial violence in Virginia Beach.

We must address the plight of thousands of southern workers who have been left without jobs because their employers have fled to Taiwan, Mexico, or the Phillipines, where wages are even cheaper, working conditions even worse, and workers even more powerless. We must somehow confront the fact that thousands of men, women, and children are homeless in the great cities of our New South.

Recent recognition and even appreciation of the massive cultural diversity that constitutes the South and American society in general have taken on a variety of forms, including changes in the curricula of our schools. But with these new and exciting changes have come reactions to that change. It is these reactions that we as anthropologists must confront in and outside our classrooms. And we must not restrict our focus to the South. Because we are the South, and the South—historically and culturally—is in us.

This means that we must speak out against bigotry, intolerance, and racism in every city, every neighborhood in the South. And we must confront all the hidden as well as obvious forms of these distorted beliefs and actions. But racism is not the private possession of the South. Witness what has happened in recent times in the North: the murder of Yusef Hawkins in Bensonhurst, Brooklyn and police killings of 14-year-old Jose Lebron and 17-year-old Louis Liranso of Brooklyn and 13-year-old David Aupont, a recent Haitian immigrant to New York. And yes, we must remember the Howard Beach racial killing. We must condemn the illegal and racist dragnet used in Mission Hill, Boston, to round up nonwhite suspects after the Stuart murder. And, unfortunately, the list goes on.

At the same time that we condemn racial *violence,* we anthropologists have a responsibility to know about and combat the other ways in which racism is expressed in everyday American life. For example:

- One in every four African American men is in prison, on probation, or on parole (compared to one-sixteenth of whites and one-tenth of Hispanics).
- A black girl has a one in twenty-one thousand chance of receiving a Ph.D. in mathematics, engineering, or the physical sciences. But she has a one in five chance of having a baby before her twentieth birthday.
- In 1987, infant mortality for African American babies was 17.9 per thousand live births compared to 8.6 for white babies. And the United States itself lags behind *nineteen* other developed nations in terms of infant mortality.
- In central Harlem, infant mortality in 1989 was 25 per thousand live births—a figure higher than the underdeveloped countries of Cuba (with a figure of 11), Jamaica (18), Trinidad (20), and Costa Rica (18)!

As Mel Konner, one of our own Southern anthropologists, so eloquently pointed out in a *New York Times* essay, life expectancy in Bangladesh is greater than in Harlem, USA! Is it not our responsibility as anthropologists to analyze why poverty among nonwhite "minorities" is on the *increase* while poverty among white folks is declining. Why is it that 33.1 percent of all black Americans and 28.2 percent of all Hispanics were living in poverty in 1987 (both increases from 1986) compared with 10.5 percent of white Americans (representing a *decrease* from 1986)? And why is it that the gap between the rich and the poor in America is widening, not closing?

I want to again focus on the South, drawing on some of my personal experience. I was born in Jacksonville, Florida, in 1936 and grew up in the intense period of southern Jim Crowism.

- I remember the water fountains for "colored" people and for "white" people. Why, in Jacksonville, Florida, there was a cemetery for the dogs of white folks, regardless of the color of the dogs.
- I shall never forget reading out of "hand-me-down" public school textbooks—handed down to us when white kids got new ones.
- Of course, I can't forget what it felt like day after day to walk out

of the door of my home to see a beautiful park—right across the street—but to be denied the right to swim there because of the color of my skin.

- And I will never forget the fear that stiffened my body one night when, in an isolated area outside of Jacksonville, the car in which we were driving had a flat tire. When a group of white men approached us, I knew what millions of black folks have known: the dread of a lynch mob. I'm certain that what saved us was my father's ability to make it known that he was a thirty-second-degree Mason in a group of four white men, where by chance three were also Masons.

- I recall the trouble it was to always go to the bathroom at the "right times," because on a long car trip out of the South there were only a few public places for "colored folks." And very few places where we could eat. So in Jacksonville, the car would be filled with fried chicken and deviled eggs and pound cake and lemonade. When we finally reached Atlanta, a hot meal would be possible at Paschals.

- And you know, I also remember how often my middle-class folks took me places in their car so that I could avoid the back of the bus.

All of that was the "Old South." And because of the struggles of countless folks, black and white, because of the civil rights movement, that Old South is no more. Formal, legal Jim Crow is no more.

But in the New South, some of the same Old South remains. I contend that this is not a consequence of something inherent in the genes of white southern folk. Indeed, a good deal of the Old South remains in the United States. Let me refer again to the recent *Time* magazine cover story "America's Changing Colors: Beyond the Melting Pot." Much of the story focuses on enumerating the "risks" of America's changing ethnic populations. Listen to the words and the tone of this passage: "The 'browning' of America offers tremendous opportunity capitalizing on the merits of many peoples from many lands. Yet this fundamental change in the ethnic makeup of the U.S. also poses risks" (9 April 1990, 29). The remainder of the article is devoted to an elaboration of all those "risks," including a criticism of changes in curricula that view "all cultures, regardless of the grandeur or paucity of their attainments, as essentially equal." As we know too well, the media plays an instrumental role in shaping American opinion. So when *Time* seeks to frighten people about the prospect of a culturally diverse future, we as teachers-scholars must be concerned.

While we may be concerned and want to act on that concern, we may also feel overwhelmed by the sheer size of the task that lies before us. It is at this point that I would like to make some suggestions as to what we anthropologists can do.

As educators and scholars, we have a critical role to play in the shaping of ideas, beliefs, and even values. Our role is important and is potentially as pivotal as the role of television news or even *Time* magazine. But first we must become conscious of our role and the variety of resources we have at our disposal. To see ourselves as powerless is almost equivalent to being powerless. (While the reverse is not always true— to see ourselves as powerful is not all that is required to be powerful— it is a necessary step toward creating and using that power.)

Listen to a passage from a recent *Boston Globe* article that decried the lack of activism by American intellectuals in comparison to their European counterparts: "American politicians and pundits are gushing over Czechoslovak playwright/president Vaclav Havel and other intellectuals pushing change abroad, but they are deeply wary of academics at home, and most American intellectuals are only too happy to keep their opinions to themselves and their politics on campus" (Radin 1990). Noam Chomsky goes even further: "We have an extremely submissive and indoctrinated intellectual class that has sold out for wealth and prestige" (quoted in Radin 1990). Thus, if we anthropologists become actively involved in fighting the growing injustices in our part of the country and in the United States as a whole, we would be going against the tide. But that shouldn't sway us or deter us, make us timid, or allow us to turn away. On the contrary, by drawing on each other and pooling all of our diverse resources in a collective effort, we have the potential to change the character of American intellectual life. But we must first start with the basics.

In our battle against a rising tide of racism in America, the most obvious and basic response for us *is* in terms of our teaching. A lecture here and there about racism, sexism, or other forms of inequality will not do. Rather, we must work to make the analysis of systems of inequality a central part of our curricula. If not in anthropology departments, then where? We must encourage open and frank discussions that go beyond simply presenting information or "facts" about these complex issues.

Through our teaching we must challenge beliefs that foster notions of inherent superiority and inferiority on the basis of biological differences. After all, who has helped the world understand the important role of culture—yes, over biology—in the human condition? The answer, of course, is that we have, anthropologists have.

As teachers we must step beyond our traditional roles in the classroom. We must move into the lives of our students and the lives of each other to discover all those parts of the puzzle that come together to form a distorted picture about other human beings. By so doing, we begin to break down the artificial barriers that exist between the academy and the community.

It is clear that we anthropologists are the scholars who have the longest tradition of scientifically studying race and the most experience with how values and behavior are learned.

But since the days of Franz Boas and Ruth Benedict, we anthropologists have not sufficiently honored our responsibility to bring our knowledge to bear on the critical social issue of racism. I think I would say that we anthropologists have *never* fully honored our responsibility to study about and struggle against racism. Interestingly, we have done far more on sexism. Indeed, feminist anthropology is where some of the most exciting theories are being crafted.

Wouldn't it be a powerful action if southern anthropologists and anthropologists in the South—the region of America most associated with racism—pioneered in a new scholarship that we might call the anthropology of racism?

We have a formidable task ahead of us. We must come closer together as teachers and southerners, as Americans, to achieve our goals. Because it is not just this generation or even this century of students that we will affect. Rather we have the task, indeed the opportunity, to influence a whole new century of American society that is less than ten years away. We can affect generations that will be citizens of that much talked about twenty-first century.

Now, who is going to do all that must be done? We might even ask, who is going to launch the anthropology of racism—letting informed theory lead to responsible social action?

African Americans
in the South

Introduction: Economic Survival, Health Maintenance, and Religious Identity in the South

Hans A. Baer and Yvonne Jones

Despite the oppressive and hard conditions of slavery, the dashed hopes of Reconstruction, the disenfranchisement of the Jim Crow era, and the significant but limited gains of the civil rights movement, African Americans have played and continue to play a significant role in the history and culture of the South. Over half of African Americans still reside in the South. While about 12 percent of the U.S. populace consists of African Americans, they account for between 12.0 percent (Texas) and 35.2 percent (Mississippi) of the population of the various southern states. Given the fact that African Americans have undergone their development as the single largest ethnic minority in the United States under mercantile and later industrial capitalism, we felt that issues of race, class, and gender stratification have played pivotal roles in their struggles for social justice, equity, and cultural identity.

The idea for the 1990 Southern Anthropological Society (SAS) Key Symposium and this volume emerged out of our discussions while participating in a four-week National Endowment for the Humanities Institute on African American Culture at Trenton State College, under the directorship of Gloria Dickinson, during the summer of 1987. Of the twenty-seven participants in the institute, we were the only two anthropologists. In the course of our many conversations, we observed that while African Americans have played and continue to play a highly significant role in the history and culture of the South, none of the key symposia of the Southern Anthropological Society since its formation in 1966 had focused on African Americans in the South. Nevertheless, we were cognizant that anthropologists had over the years delivered papers in key symposia and other sessions of the SAS on African Americans and that there has been a long-standing tradition of anthropological research on African Americans in the South. We felt that the need for a key symposium on African Americans was long overdue and were pleased when the SAS board not only accepted our proposal but selected Atlanta, the major metropolis in the South and a city that has played a pivotal role in African American history, as the site for the 1990 SAS annual meeting.

From an academic perspective, Atlanta was a logical site for the me‹ting because it is the home of several historic black institutions of higher education, namely Atlanta University, Morehouse College, Spelman College, Morris Brown, Clark College, and the Interdenominational Theological Center, which are organized into a consortium called the Atlanta University Center. Atlanta University served as the base for W. E. B. DuBois's scholarly studies both as the seat of his professorship there and through a series of conferences between 1898 and 1930 that summarized research and public policy regarding the economic, political, and sociocultural conditions of African Americans in the South. "The proceedings of each Atlanta University conference were published, and together they constitute the beginning of modern applied research on the black experience. This work was the early origin of black studies" (Alkalimat 1986:8). In 1940, DuBois founded *Phylon: A Journal of Race and Culture* at Atlanta University. He edited it from 1940 to 1944.

Whereas DuBois lent his academic credentials to the eminence of Atlanta as a center of black higher education during the early decades of the twentieth century, anthropologist Johnnetta Cole has donated hers in the 1980s and 1990s as the dynamic president of Spelman College. In keeping with her spellbinding style, she presented a stirring keynote address before the combined audiences of the American Ethnological Society and the Southern Anthropological Society. Her remarks, which stand as the foreword to this volume, set the tone for the Key Symposium, which convened in sessions before and after her address on 27 April 1990.

While we solicited papers on a variety of topics relating to African Americans in the South, we requested our contributors to frame their presentations around the issues of race, class, and gender. Within this larger context, essays in this volume fall into three major categories:

strategies of economic survival, health and reproduction problems, and religious responses to the larger society. Brett Williams, who served as a discussant at the 1990 SAS Key Symposium, provides a critical but constructive epilogue to the essays in this volume.

In the first two papers of this volume, Annie S. Barnes and Charles Williams and Hilda J. B. Williams discuss two strategies that African Americans have embarked upon in addressing their economic survival in the larger society. Under mercantile capitalism and slavery, most African Americans were regarded as a form of property used for profit-making either on plantations or in factories and other commercial enterprises. Following the Civil War, the freed people became transformed initially into a rural peasantry. As American society underwent industrialization and urbanization, an increasing number of blacks underwent a process of proletarianization. These changes in the political economy prompted the migration of masses of rural blacks into the cities of both the North and the South. In the North, industrialists used black workers as strike-breakers to crush the growing strength of labor unions. This practice, coupled with the racially discriminatory policies of both corporations and labor unions, resulted in the creation of a split-labor market, under which whites were employed as skilled workers and blacks as semi-skilled or unskilled workers (Bonacich 1976; Marks 1981). Within this arrangement, blacks were the last to be hired and the first to be fired.

Furthermore, within the context of the split-labor market, most black women have experienced triple exploitation. As Alkalimat (1986:218) observes, "Class (economic) exploitation, racism, and sexist oppression have combined to put Black women at the bottom rung on most measures of social equality: below white males, Black males, and most white females." The National Urban League (1983) reports that whereas the mean incomes for full-time white male workers, black male workers, and white female workers in 1980 were $21,023, $14,709, and $12,156, respectively, the mean income for full-time black female workers was $11,230. Whereas 37.9 percent of white males, 22.1 percent of black males, and 28.8 percent of white females had one or more years of college education, only 20.6 percent of black women had achieved the same level of education.

Though they are only 11.4% of the female work force, Black women comprise 65% of all maids, 63% of all household cooks, 41% of all housekeepers, and 34% of all cleaning service workers. Conversely, Black women represent only 4% of all women lawyers and doctors and 5.5% of all women college teachers. Clearly, Black women (along with Black men) have provided U.S. capitalism with essential labor in some of the hardest, lowest-paying, and dirtiest jobs of all the necessary "shit work" of an advanced capitalist society. (Alkalimat 1986:218)

Since slavery, proportionately more black women have worked outside of their homes than have white women. Furthermore, as Angela Davis (1981:231) observes, most black women have "carried the double burden of wage labor and housework." During World War II, tens of thousands of black women went into jobs previously held by men. Many unemployed black men, desperate for work, regarded their wives' ability to obtain employment as a comment on their own masculinity. Although both black men and women were negatively affected by the split-labor market, sexism drove a wedge between them. Many black men encouraged their wives and daughters to return to traditional domestic tasks and bear children "for the race." Even outside of marriage, the number of black children born since World War II increased dramatically. As Annie S. Barnes notes in her essay, teenage pregnancy has become a major issue confronting the African American community. The roots of black teenage pregnancy are complex but must ultimately be viewed within the context of racial, class, and gender relations in American society. The subordinate status of black female adolescents resulting from systematic tripartite discrimination inevitably creates in many of them feelings of low self-esteem. Given their seemingly hopeless situation, a large number of poor black teenage females attempt to boost their self-esteem by bearing a child—a child that symbolizes their womanhood, humanity, and capacity to love and be loved by others. Tragically, their desperate search for human dignity within the harsh reality of the American political economy even further limits their opportunities to obtain an education and occupational skills. Ultimately, the dilemmas faced by both poor black teenage boys and girls will require drastic structural changes in American society.

In their essay, Charles Williams and Hilda J. B. Williams discuss the creation of mutual aid societies, one form of voluntary association, by African Americans as they attempted to adjust to the vissicitudes of racism, segregation, and economic marginality both in rural areas of the South and urban areas of both the North and the South. While undoubtedly voluntary associations often play a compensatory role, Kerri (1976:417) maintains that they should be viewed primarily as "a rational decision to overcome the restrictive conditions imposed by the larger society." Black voluntary associations are quite diverse in their activities and purposes. In Louisville, Kentucky, Seals and Kolaja (1964:27–32) identified 211 black voluntary associations, most of which were in either church or church-related activities or were social or recreational in nature. Some mutual aid societies developed into life insurance companies, banks, savings and loan firms, and mortgage companies. These black-owned businesses tend to be concentrated in southern cities. Despite the existence of such traditional black businesses as well as the appearance of new ones, the future for black capitalism appears grim with the growing trend toward corporate concentration. Black businesses are generally situated in the competitive sector as opposed to the monopoly sector of the American economy and account for a tiny portion of the U.S. gross national product (GNP). "Black business firms' receipts totaled 0.46 percent of the GNP in 1972 but was [*sic*] down to 0.39 percent in 1985. Economist Andrew Brimmer . . . notes, for example, that receipts from black businesses equaled 13.5 percent of the total black income in 1969 and only 8.9 percent in 1980. If current trends continue, the black share may drop to 7 percent by 1990" (Bullard 1989:169).

In the next three essays, Carole E. Hill, Holly F. Mathews, and Ira E. Harrison discuss problems in the area of health and access to health care faced by African Americans in the South. Hill observes that African Americans in the South find themselves victimized in these areas on at least three counts: as southerners, as members of a racial minority, and for most as members of a lower class. As a region and, historically, as a semicolony of northern capital, the South has the lowest health status in the United States. While Hill and Mathews focus on access to health care, the poor health profile of southern blacks must also be related to the social production of illness due to the harsh working conditions in the southern states, with their "right-to-work" (or what we prefer to term "right-to-exploit") laws and weak environmental protection laws.

In the Institute for Southern Studies' "Green Score Card," based on a poisons index, a public health index, a worker health index, and a politics and policies index, southern states take the bottom slots in every category (Hall 1990). Louisiana ranked fiftieth on the poisons index, Mississippi on the public health and worker health indices, Arkansas on the politics and policies index, and Alabama on the overall Green rank.

> The region has six of the ten states with the highest per capita amounts of toxic chemical discharge, seven of the ten producing the most hazardous waste, 92 of the 149 facilities that pose the greatest risk of cancer to their neighbors, and 30 of the top 100 industrial sources of ozone-depleting chemicals.
> The South also has six of the ten states with the highest unemployment rates, seven of the ten with the lowest rates of health insurance protection, and nine of the ten with the highest rates of premature deaths. Ten of the South's 13 states already have above average incident rates of cancer, and we're catching up fast with the higher rates of the more poisoned Rustbelt. (Hall 1990:51–52)

Working-class people, both black and white, as well as many middle-class blacks, often reside in neighborhoods adjacent to industrial plants and toxic waste sites, making them particularly prone to contract environmentally related diseases (Bullard and Wright 1986).

Under slavery many slaveowners provided medical care for their slaves since the latter constituted a financial investment necessary for the production of capital. After the Civil War, however, African Americans generally became responsible for their own health care. African American ethnomedicine apparently emerged into full fruition during this period. As Puckett (1926:167) observes, when "the treatment of disease was taken out of the hands of the master and given again to the Negroes, their desire to avoid expensive medical attention focused their attention again on the all-powerful 'root doctor' or 'hoodoo-man' as the healer of disease." In her essay, Hill points out that black southerners have historically resorted and continue to resort to a variety of healers in attempting to cope with the inequities that racism and class stratification have created in the delivery of biomedicine. These include independent specialists, such as the herbalist and the granny midwife; independent generalists, such as the conjurer or rootworker; cultic specialists, such as the evangelical faith healer or the messianic-nationalist divine healer; and cultic generalists, such as the voodoo priest or priestess and the Spiritual prophet (Baer 1982).

In her essay, Mathews discusses the disappearance of the granny midwife in North Carolina, in large part because of restrictive legislation that pushed them out of practice (see Dougherty 1982). In contrast to other African American folk healers, the granny midwife worked under the supervision of a medical doctor, generally a white one. The biomedical establishment and state health agencies have discriminated against granny midwives as members of a triple minority, namely as poor black women. In working for white male physicians, granny midwives functioned under systems of both racial and gender hierarchy. These arrangements pose the question as to why more granny midwives did not work under the supervision of black physicians as well.

In essence, institutional racism in both the South and North greatly restricted the training of black physicians. Since the closure of nine of eleven black medical schools between 1882 and 1923, the vast majority of practicing black physicians in the United States have graduated from two medical schools, Howard University College of Medicine (established in 1868) and Meharry Medical School (established in 1876) (Savitt 1984:162). The Flexner Report, conducted in 1910, played a significant role in closing five of the existing black medical schools and all but one of the existing women's medical schools (Berliner 1985). In the process, biomedicine became transformed into a white male upper-class and upper-middle-class preserve. "By 1938–39 only 22 of 77 medical schools in the United States admitted black students. In 1955–56 the numbers had changed to 50 of 82 schools, and in 1961–62 a total of 57 of 85 schools admitted black students. In 1970–71, 21 medical schools still had no black students" (Jones and Rice 1987:11). In 1979 the Medical School at Morehouse College in Atlanta became the third predominantly black medical school in the United States.

Because the American Medical Association (AMA) did not admit blacks prior to 1964, black physicians created the National Medical Association (NMA) in 1895. Unlike the AMA, the NMA has been a strong advocate of national health insurance, in part because black physicians sought financial reimbursement to compensate for their lower incomes relative to their white counterparts (Jackson 1981:41). Although about 53 percent of African Americans reside in the South, only 32 percent of active black physicians practice there (Gray 1976). Indeed racism and professional exclusion from white medical societies and white hospitals prompted many black physicians to flee the South for the North or West. Like their white counterparts, black medical students were socialized into the reductionist biomedical theory of disease, which downplayed the social origins of illness and tended to blame the victim for his or her health problems. As Beardsley (1987:150) aptly observes, "Negro medical students, even at black colleges, were subjected to the view that the Negro race was a sick race and that its ills were grounded either in wasteful living or in some inherent physiological weakness."

A disproportionate number of persons with AIDS have been blacks and Hispanics. Furthermore, minority groups survive for a shorter period after having been diagnosed as having AIDS than do whites with the disease, in part due to the inequities in access to health care as a result of racism and class stratification in American society. According to Friedman and his colleagues, "there has been little mobilization by minority communities or organizations to come to grips with AIDS. This lack of minority mobilization has undoubtedly been furthered by the fact that black and Hispanic gays were more stigmatized and less organized than white gays before the advent of the epidemic, and by the hostility of many minority institutions and leaders to intravenous (IV) drug users" (Friedman et al. 1987:456). In his essay, Ira Harrison discusses the resistance of one black institution, namely the black church, to confronting AIDS in the African American community of a medium-sized southern city. Although many southern black churches, particularly of the Baptist and Methodist varieties, served as backbone of the civil rights movement, their evangelical morality prevents them from offering solace to the plight of AIDS victims. As a result, concerned blacks in Happy Valley have had to create secular support groups that rely on expertise from the white-dominated medical establishment.

Diet has always been essential to health maintenance in all sociocultural groups. While, as Tony L. Whitehead notes in his essay, African American foodways are often cited as a cause of a variety of black health problems, particularly cardiovascular ones, poverty has been a major determinant of the foods that blacks consume. When a nurse chided an elderly Charleston black woman for not feeding her children as recommended, she replied, "I sho' wish I could give 'em the sorta food you tell me they ought to have. . . . But best I can do is giv 'em 'nough to keep 'em from starving" (quoted in Beardsley 1987:30). Nevertheless, as Whitehead demonstrates, African American foodways are quite variable and a result of complex sociocultural processes that often provide a balanced diet, particularly in rural areas. Religious affiliation and alternative lifestyles also shape foodways among African Americans: "For example, members of the American Muslim Mission . . . abstain from consuming pork and alcoholic beverages. Conforming Seventh Day Adventists also do not eat pork. Some blacks are vegetarians" (Jackson 1981:110).

In the last three essays of this volume, Hans A. Baer, Merrill Singer, and Daryl White and O. Kendall White discuss the involvement of African Americans in three distinctly religious movements, namely Pentecostalism, Judaism, and Mormonism. Despite the emergence of a few independent black denominations in the North, such as the African Methodist Episcopal Church and the African Methodist Episcopal Zion Church during the early 1800s, the roots of institutionalized religion among African Americans essentially are in the South. Most southern blacks joined Baptist and Methodist churches—either black congregations affiliated with white-controlled denominations or independent black congregations. Furthermore, some free blacks belonged to black congregations affiliated with the white-controlled Episcopalian and Presbyterian churches. Changes in the political economy of the United States coupled with the onset of World War I resulted in the massive migration of African Americans from the rural South to the cities of the North and, to a lesser degree, to the cities of the South. The process of urbanization that accompanies capitalist expansion has repeatedly been demonstrated to have unsettling effects on rural migrants. Invariably, rural migrants worldwide attempt to adjust to their new environment, as Charles Williams points out in his essay, by creating a wide array of voluntary associations, including religious ones. Although storefront versions of the large National Baptist congregations, and to a lesser extent, the African Methodist congregations were established, many black migrants were attracted to the Holiness, Pentecostal, Spiritual, Judaic, Islamic, and other sects, such as the father Divine Peace Mission and the African Orthodox Church. These emerged in tremendous profusion not only in the industrial North, but, as Baer and Singer note in their essays, also in many southern towns and cities. The Great Depression accelerated the process of religious diversification. According to Wilmore (1983:163), "the black community, by the end of the decade of the 1930s, was literally glutted with churches of every variety and description."

In large measure, African American sects emerged as religious responses to racism and social stratification in the larger society (Baer and Singer 1981). All black religious groups to a greater or lesser degree have juxtaposed elements of protest and accommodation to the social structure of American society. Although the black mainstream denominations, namely the National Baptist and the Black Methodist bodies, have exhibited accommodative dimensions, they have, at least in theory and often in action, been committed to a reformist program of social activism that would enable blacks to become better integrated into the political, economic, and social institutions of the larger society. Although most black mainstream congregations stood on the sidelines of the events that followed the Supreme Court school desegregation decision of 1954, many black mainstream ministers and congregations joined the civil rights movement. Needless to say, Dr. Martin Luther King, Jr., a young, middle-class Baptist minister with an affinity for the Social Gospel and Gandhian nonviolence, became a pivotal figure in that movement—and with his assassination, its most poignant symbol. As Morris (1984) observes, King's Southern Christian Leadership Conference served as "the decentralized political arm of the black church" in the struggle for civil rights.

In contrast to the mainstream denominations, messianic-nationalist groups rejected integration into the larger society and advocated the creation of separate utopian communities committed to a strong concept of black nationhood. While Black Muslim sects, which generally emerged in northern ghettos, generally have received the greatest attention, Black Judaism historically constitutes another stream of messianic-nationalism. As Singer notes in his essay, although Black Judaism came to its fullest fruition in the North, its origins are steeped in the South and can be traced back to the close identification that slaves felt to the bondage that the ancient Israelites experienced in Pharonic Egypt.

Next to the black mainstream denominations, the conversionist sects, which consist primarily of a great multitude of Holiness and Pentecostal congregations and organizations, appear to be the largest religious grouping among African Americans. Conversionist sects characteristically adopt an expressive strategy of social action, emphasizing the importance of various behavioral patterns, such as shouting, ecstatic dancing, and speaking in tongues as outward manifestations of "sanctification." In their initial stages, conversionist sects tend to be otherworldly and apolitical in their orientation, and rely upon the willingness of the individual to undergo a process of personal conversion as the means to affect social transformation. Yet, as Baer maintains in his essays, at least one conversionist sect—namely the Church of God in Christ, which emerged in Mississippi and has been headquartered since 1907 in Memphis, Tennessee—has begun to undergo a process of denominationalization, including a greater affinity toward social reform programs and middle-class value orientations.

While about 90 percent of church-going African Americans belong to black-controlled religious organizations, the remaining 10 percent or so belong to white-controlled religious organizations. The "ambiguous position" of middle-class African Americans prompted many of them to join the Presbyterian, Congregational, and Episcopal churches, and in more recent decades the Catholic, United Methodist, and even Southern Baptist churches (Frazier 1974:83–84). Furthermore, as White and White demonstrate in their essay, an increasing number of blacks have been joining the Mormon Church, including those in the South, a region characterized by fundamentalist antipathy to "cults," such as Mormonism. While a small number of blacks belonged to the Mormon Church during the period when it had an official ban on blacks entering its priesthood, the lifting of the ban has encouraged some blacks to join what is an overwhelmingly white religious organization and a bastion of middle-class conservatism, familism, patriarchy, and respectability.

Anthropological research on African Americans in the South can be traced to Zora Neale Hurston's (1935) collection of black folklore in her home state of Florida and apprenticeship as a voodoo practitioner in New Orleans during the 1920s and to the community studies of black-white relations in Mississippi conducted by Hortense Powdermaker (1939) and Allison Davis, Burleigh Davis, and Mary R. Gardner (1941). Since their seminal studies, many anthropologists have conducted research on southern blacks, including ethnographies of black communities (see Kunkel and Kennard 1971; Dougherty 1978b; Thomas 1986). The essays in this volume serve as examples of ongoing anthropological research on African Americans in the South and, we hope, will stimulate more anthropologists and other social scientists to conduct fieldwork on this populace.

While many southern blacks continue to live in rural areas, most today live in urban areas. Over the course of the twentieth century, the majority of African Americans have been transformed from a rural

peasantry into an urban proletariat. As a result of the civil rights movement, a significant number of blacks in both the South and other regions
of the country entered the middle class. Since the passage of the Voting
Rights Act of 1965, the number of black elected officials, of which many
hold office in the South, soared from one hundred to sixty-seven hundred (Marable 1990:22). In November 1989, Douglas Wilder, a black,
was elected governor of Virginia. Despite these impressive gains, the
existence of a black underclass has endured into the 1990s. Sociologist
William J. Wilson (1987) argues that the African American underclass
continues economically to fall behind both middle-class African Americans and European Americans.

During the 1970s, southern corporate elites and politicians made con-
certed efforts to eradicate the image of the South as an economically
underdeveloped region and proclaimed the emergence of yet another
"New South."

> However, many of the problems that characterized the postindustrial econ-
> omy endured in southern metropolises. Emerging industries and technical
> fields did not provide a major source of new jobs for the blacks who were
> concentrated in the central cities. Both in-migrants and incumbent resi-
> dents of the region who had marginal skills generally found themselves in
> the growing unemployment lines. Individuals who did not have the requi-
> site education often became part of the emerging underclass. The new
> prosperity in the South heightened status differentials between blacks and
> whites. The shift of population and jobs to the suburbs contributed to the
> ghettoization of central-city blacks and exacerbated many existing social
> problems. . . . Poverty in the South represented a source of "cheap labor."
> (Bullard 1989:2)

Since the 1960s, despite electoral victories on the part of black candidates, an increasing number of African Americans have felt themselves
alienated from the corporate-controlled, two-party political system.
While many blacks voted in the Democratic party primaries in 1984
and again, along with a significant number of whites, in 1988 for Jesse
Jackson, the Democratic party has consistently distanced itself from
the leader of the Rainbow Coalition. During the 1980s, an increasing
number of Americans, including African Americans, joined grass-roots
organizations that challenge the economic interests of corporations and
question the ability of corporate-backed politicians to represent the general will of the people. Ultimately, the issues of race, class, and gender

that have historically had an adverse impact on African Americans in the South and the United States as a whole must be viewed within the context of late capitalism. Bearing this in mind, hopefully we will draw inspiration from Johnnetta Cole's plea, in the foreword to this volume, calling upon southern anthropologists and anthropologists in the South to engage in the anthropology of racism. We hope the essays in this volume will contribute to that effort and the demystification of a political economy that exploits African Americans on the basis of race, class, or gender.

African American Teen Pregnancy in the American South

Annie S. Barnes

This essay will examine three outcomes of African American teenage pregnancy: live births, induced abortions, and natural fetal deaths in the American South. According to the 1988 projected population of the American South, African Americans comprise 17.9 percent of the total population in the seventeen southern states while other minorities comprise 1.7 percent. In this paper I will be mainly concerned with African American teen pregnancy. Pregnancies are the sum of live births, induced abortions, and natural fetal deaths. The findings indicate that the number of African American teen mothers is sizeable. They also indicate that racism and sexism are major contributors to the prevalence of African American adolescent pregnancy, while an intervening cause is low self-esteem; it is, therefore, a complex pattern of behavior. Another conclusion of this study is that more effort needs to be placed on eradicating racism, sexism, and low self-esteem as they relate to African American female teens in order to reduce the large number of African American teenage pregnancies in the southern states. It will be easier to promote high self-esteem than to eliminate entrenched racism and sexism within the society.

While tremendous gains have been made by African Americans in the attainment of equality of opportunity in the American South, serious problems persist. These impact all generations of African American females, including teens; hence, the widespread existence of teen motherhood must be understood in the context of a broader problem. The problem is the practice of institutional racism designed to perpetuate the "social disorganization" of African American family life (Ladner 1972:5). For example, white racism has established an exploitative economic system (Staples 1973:5–6). In this regard, Rainwater

(1970:424), noted that the American underclass "is created by, and its existence is maintained by, the operation of what is in other ways the most successful economic system known to man." It is this deprivation of African Americans that results in marginal and alienating behavior, including teen parenthood. Thus, inequality in the economic system is at the heart of the problem (Rainwater 1970:424).

The nature of the inequality is clear. According to Marshall (1977: 62), whites and some African Americans themselves are motivated to discriminate against African Americans on the basis of status, job, and other factors. It follows that we should ask who discriminates? According to Walker (1973:24), hiring officials discriminate against African Americans by utilizing test results to place job applicants in the unqualified category. Whites also use "aptitude or intelligence tests, without proving their relationship to predicting successful job performance" (Feagin and Feagin 1978:58). Another way that hiring officials have kept African Americans from getting jobs is by hiring whites and paying them higher wages (Becker 1957:3, 6). Also, white employees discriminate in the economic system against African Americans by forcing employers to discriminate in hiring practices (Alexis 1974:73–74). Moreover, white customers discriminate against African Americans by "paying higher prices to buy from whites" (Alexis 1974:81). According to Barnes (1986:14–15), when this occurs, employers earn enough to pay higher wages to employ whites and yet make a profit, which results in an increase in the unemployment rate among African Americans. The overall effect is that a large number of owners of production as well as some white workers and consumers discriminate against African Americans in the economic institution, but African American women are at the greatest disadvantage. For example, "unemployment is more severe among Black women than among Black men or White women and nonwhite girls have the highest rate of unemployment" (Pressman 1970:104). And even among employed African Americans, white racism is at work. African American female employees experience differential treatment in jobs, duties, amount of work assigned, number of working hours, wages, raises, and promotions (Barnes 1986:35).

Not only does white racism result in economic exploitation, but it also creates an African American subculture characterized among the masses by male-female interpersonal conflict (Staples 1973:5). This is made clear in the behavior of African American unwed parents. Instead of them closing ranks, their daily contact with institutional racism causes them to "become victims of the divide-and-conquer strategy of their real enemy—White racism and its agents" (Staples 1973:5). For example, when African American unmarried teens become parents, the male and female teens find themselves at great odds; frequently the girl desires marriage, but the male usually does not oblige (Barnes 1987). In fact, he is often unable to provide economic support for the child and emotional support for the mother (Barnes 1990:97–98); as a result their relationship becomes splintered.

Hence, the deterioration of the social environment created by white racism causes many African American families to splinter under oppression. For example, as early as 1975, the number of children born to unmarried African American women reached 250,000, 48.8 percent of all births to African American women (Marable 1984:175).

This conflict uncovers another pattern of behavior, sexism, also created by economic inequality and white racism. What we must understand is that African American males want success, and when racism denies them opportunity, they seek other means of achievement, including sexist ones. Exaggerated male virility is a substitution, though a poor one, for achievement; or, to say it another way, sexism is the "exploitation of females, individually or as a group, by males" (Rothenberg 1988:21). Exploitation may take many forms. Hence, it was found in multiple cases in Tidewater, Virginia, in 1981, that conceptions of African American male virility lead to frequent sex, a child, and children as proof of manhood (Barnes 1987:39). When some African American males are denied ordinary masculine identity, sex becomes a major instrument of power, a weapon against their own women (Bernard 1966:76). Thus, even though unmarried, most teen males are "proud" to be fathers (Dougherty 1978b:89). Consequently, the virility cult among African American men exploits African American females and continues a divide-and-conquer strategy that plays into the pattern of white racism. As Vontress (1971:15) has said, the emasculation of African American men has caused them to seek manhood in secondary aspects of masculinity, particularly exploitation of African American women. The virility cult among street-corner men makes them eager to exploit women sexually and economically and leads them to expect the same behavior from other men (Liebow 1967:143). Staples (1973:57) notes how African American females suffer from this virility cult: "One woman complained that the Black man spends too much time trying to prove that he is the great lover that he is accused of being by the white man."

Interestingly, there is a solution to racism and sexism. It can be accomplished when African Americans and whites overcome myths and legends, fears and prejudices, and the economic and social fruits of the society are made available to all (Davis, Gardner, and Gardner 1941:x).

This goal should be encouraged because racism and sexism promote a lack of respect for African American females. According to Powdermaker (1939:369), "Perhaps the most severe result of denying respect to an individual is the insidious effect on his self-esteem." Powdermaker continues, "Few can long resist self-doubt in the face of constant belittling and humiliation at the hands of others." Ladner (1972:81) concurs and says that racism has programmed social, cultural, political, and economic institutions to espouse alleged inferiority of African Americans. Both racism and sexism impact directly the lives of black teens. It is vivid in their sexual behavior. Because they want to be respected, because they want to be loved, because they want to become somebody, African American females become exploited by men's "begging" for sex (Barnes 1987:38). However, perhaps the most telling example of what a denial of respect does to African American females is reported by Dougherty. Dougherty (1978b:82) found that "most girls do not talk about 'love.' They speak about 'being crazy' about a man, meaning that they cannot keep their mind off of him, feel that they want him permanently and would 'do anything' to 'get him.'" Without racism and sexism, African American female teens would likely have higher regard for themselves, refrain from sex, or utilize effective contraceptives with selected males and seek economic and social success, not babies. However, it must be emphasized that most African American single mothers do not have more than one child (Barnes 1989:50–52). When racism, sexism, and low self-esteem are eradicated, the numbers of children born to teen mothers will decrease.

METHODOLOGY

For purposes of this study, the American South is comprised of the states of Alabama, Arkansas, Delaware, Florida, Georgia, Kentucky,

Louisiana, Maryland, Mississippi, Missouri, North Carolina, Oklahoma, South Carolina, Tennessee, Texas, Virginia, and West Virginia. All minority teenage mothers are included in the data from each state, except Florida, Georgia, Missouri, and Maryland, which provided information only about African American teenage mothers.

In each state the appropriate department responsible for compiling statistical information about minority teenage pregnancies provided printed materials and statistical reports. Supervisors and employees of adolescent care and health departments provided written and telephone pregnancy rationale reports, especially for this paper. The question that I asked each state's representative informant was: What do you perceive to be the causes of African American teen pregnancy in your particular state? The data collection process lasted from May 1989 to February 1990.

PROFILE OF AFRICAN AMERICAN TEENAGE MOTHERS IN THE SOUTH

The data obtained from the southern states are used to examine three outcomes of African American teenage pregnancy: live births, induced abortions, and natural fetal deaths. The live birth data were taken from the latest statistical reports available in the American South. Fourteen states provided the number of live births to minority teenage mothers in 1987, while two states provided data for minority teens in 1988, and one state provided data for live births in 1984. The difference in reporting years is not judged significant enough to distort analysis. Even though the statistical information comes from different years, only one year's data is reported for each state. Hence, references are made to a "one-year period" in this essay. By combining the data available from each state on minority teenage births, we determined the total number of births over a year's time (see Table 1). There were 73,547 births to minority teens in the seventeen southern states in a one-year period. A possible explanation for differences in live births in the southern region is location of the population. When the states were ranked, the nine states with the highest number of live births in a year's time were usually located in the Deep South. The young minority mothers in the seventeen states ranged from age 10 to 19. Of the 73,547 births, 3,243 were to

Table 1
Minority (Age 10–19) Live Births in the South

Southern States	Year	No.	Rank
Florida[a]	1987	9,937	1
Georgia[a]	1987	8,267	2
Louisiana	1987	6,966	3
North Carolina	1987	6,906	4
Mississippi	1987	5,361	5
Alabama	1987	5,071	6
Maryland[a]	1987	4,589	7
South Carolina	1987	4,707	8
Texas	1987	4,655	9
Virginia	1987	4,345	10
Tennessee	1984	3,655	11
Missouri[a]	1988	3,351	12
Arkansas	1987	2,331	13
Oklahoma	1987	1,280	14
Kentucky	1987	1,197	15
Delaware[a]	1987	613	16
West Virginia	1988	199	17
Total		73,547	

Sources: The states' vital statistical reports and printouts.
[a]African Americans only

mothers under age 15 (4.4 percent) and 70,304 (95.6 percent) were to minority mothers aged 15 to 19.

Only nine states—Arkansas, Georgia, Louisiana, Mississippi, Missouri, North Carolina, South Carolina, Tennessee, and Virginia—reported data on induced abortions. The five states, in ranked order, with the highest number of induced abortions among minority teenage mothers are North Carolina, Georgia, Virginia, South Carolina, and Missouri. In 1987 there were 16,927 induced abortions among minority teens in these nine states. Among young teens, under age 15, there was variation, by state, in the number of abortions. The variation is seen in their ranked order. A larger number of young minority teens in Mississippi had abortions in 1987 than in any of the other eight southern states. The remaining eight states ranked in this order: Louisiana, Tennessee,

Arkansas, Missouri and North Carolina, Virginia, South Carolina, and Georgia. A slightly different ranking existed for minority teens between the ages of 15 and 19. Hence, Georgia ranked first in abortions among minority teens 15 to 19 years of age. The order of frequency of abortions in the remaining eight states was South Carolina, Virginia, Missouri and North Carolina, Arkansas, Tennessee, Louisiana, and Mississippi. In the nine states overall, there were 1,317 abortions in a one-year period among minority teens under age 15, and 15,610 abortions among minority teens aged 15 to 19 during the same time span.

As indicated earlier, teenage pregnancy also includes outcomes of fetal deaths. Fetal deaths are synonymous with miscarriages and spontaneous abortions. Sixteen of the southern states provided information on fetal deaths. During a one-year period, there were 1,564 fetal deaths to pregnant minority adolescents in these states. Ranked in order from highest frequency were Georgia, Virginia, Florida, Arkansas, Mississippi, Louisiana, Maryland, and Alabama and North Carolina, which tied. Sixteen of the seventeen southern states provided the number of fetal deaths to minority teenage women under age 15. In one year, they experienced a total of ninety-four fetal deaths. The five states, in order of rank, that had the highest number of fetal deaths to minority teens under age 15 were Georgia, Florida, Virginia, Mississippi, and Louisiana. However, of the ninety-four fetal deaths, twenty-five occurred in Georgia and thirteen in Virginia. Delaware and Texas did not report any fetal deaths to minority teens under age 15. Sixteen states also provided information on fetal deaths among minority teens aged 15 to 19. There were 1,470 fetal deaths reported for this age group. The five states that experienced fetal deaths among teenage minorities most frequently, in order of rank, were Georgia, Virginia, Florida, Arkansas, and Mississippi.

When the maternal specialists for teens in the seventeen southern states were asked the rationale for pregnancy in their own state, they provided specific ideas. According to these maternal specialists, African American teen pregnancy in the American South involves complex sets of linked factors that occur in females' experiences. One linkage is poverty and lack of education—poor academic skills and absence or lack of adequate family-life education in schools. Another linkage is poverty and high unemployment. In this regard, a teen consultant noted that successful females should be studied and those findings applied to the education of minority children living in poverty. Such an approach should help eliminate the double jeopardy of institutionalized racism and sexism.

Thirteen of the maternal specialists in the seventeen southern states found that deficits in ego functioning lead to early sexual behavior and increased risk of pregnancy. Low self-esteem is evident in the teens' belief that they cannot achieve other goals. Other factors include unstable family relationships; the need to love or fear of not being loved; and the need to have somebody, a baby, to love. Other factors that indicate deficits in the ego are competition with the mother or significant other, punishment of a father or mother, the wish for emancipation from perceived or actual undesirable home situations, the need for attention, an attempt to control people or situations, and a lack of future orientation. Moreover, the informants reported other signals of low self-esteem, for example, possible added status from the ability to father a child or become pregnant. For many teens who live in alcoholic and drug-abusive homes, sex might substitute for the lack of physical closeness. In effect, some teens with low self-esteem see sex as an expression of love for the male and an expression of the male's love for them as well as a rite of passage to womanhood.

Another factor related to the minority teens' sexual activity is that low self-esteem along with lack of responsibility is evident in the failure of teens to use birth control consistently and correctly. Perhaps the most vivid example of low self-esteem is some teens' desire for a man's baby as a souvenir following the breakup of a relationship (Barnes 1987:40). Still another suggested cause of pregnancy is intense female sex desire without corresponding use of contraception. These observations indicate that African American teens are an oppressed group with the need to build self-esteem. Writing a status report for the Urban League of America, McMurray reaches the same conclusion. She states, "Building self-esteem then should be a key theme in providing services for Black adolescents and most particularly for those from economically and emotionally impoverished circumstances" (1990:207). As noted above, low self-esteem often results from structural inequalities that lead to the exploitation and oppression of persons in minority status. Ultimately, extensive societal change is called for if positive self-esteem is to be the right of all persons in the American South.

AFRICAN AMERICAN TEEN PREGNANCY
PREVENTION MODEL

In view of the influence of institutional racism and sexism on the behavior of African American females, pregnancy prevention is inextricably interwoven with structural changes that should occur in the familial, political, economic, and educational institutions. There should be a larger countertrend from single parenthood toward the two-parent family. The political system must guarantee true justice for African American teen males so that they will not turn to crime in the first instance. If they do enter the criminal justice system, they should be able to expect training and positive opportunities to pursue a successful life in their home communities. Another structural change needed in the political system is provision for funding for the express purpose of helping unwed teen mothers achieve self-sufficiency. Now is the time to reverse racism and use the political system to nurture and promote young African American males and females as it does young whites. Structural change is needed in the economic system also. Young African American males and females have a right to encouragement, jobs, and wages as readily as they are given to white youth. Equal treatment of this nature will encourage more African American males to stay off the streets and out of the courts and bedrooms, to get into the workplace and the school system. Thus, extensive structural changes must be made in the school system. These changes refer to justice and opportunities. That is, minority youth, especially African American males, deserve equal justice from security officers, teachers, and administrators in the hallways, classrooms, and school offices. Such treatment would reduce African American male suspensions and expulsions. Administrators, counselors, and teachers should implement policies that keep African American males in school, give them encouragement, and provide them with structured, in-depth teaching. Structural changes in school interaction would result in fewer African American males and females getting in trouble and becoming school dropouts and putouts. The obvious conclusion is that changes in all the major institutional structures are called for since they would contribute to improving the life chances of African Americans of the South.

Coupled with these structural changes is the need for African American teens to do something for themselves. African American males and females should fight back in the societal institutions. They can begin by recognizing differential treatment in economic institutions while working effectively, seeking out a mentor of any race, and tactfully requesting their rights. Fighting back in the school system should include daily attendance in school and exemplary behavior and school performance, while fighting against the penal system should involve the relinquishment of violence and other adverse behaviors.

Still another approach to structural constraints is to teach African American male and female teens why they are victimized by racism and how to fight back. They are victimized by whites to keep them from realizing their full potential. Rather than exhibit the behavior whites accuse them of, they should be determined to avoid such oppressive relations.

Also, African Americans need to challenge class stratification. When I asked persons in the various statistical departments about the concentration of live births to minority teenage mothers, the response was that they mainly concern low-income teens. The most oppressed group among African Americans is the poor. In effect, racism oppresses all African Americans but especially the poor who have not yet begun to fight back in ways that count. Pregnancy rates of teens from low-income families need not and should not exceed teen pregnancy on higher socioeconomic levels. Reduced adolescent pregnancy can be attained if all institutions—the family, church, community, and school—help all youth develop new goals, hope, and the desire to achieve. Young persons need help from responsible adults and other youth to learn that a college degree and a promising vocational career, for example, are preferable to a baby for attaining success both within the community and in one's own eyes.

Another avenue to pregnancy prevention is the elimination of sexism. African American males need to be taught by their families and other responsible groups not to exploit African American female youth. This can be achieved by training African American males to respect African American womanhood and to recognize that becoming a man means accepting responsibility for females as well as for themselves. Moreover, families and community groups can help African American males to avoid sexism by helping them set high yet achievable educational, occupational, and income goals. Further, African American males should be taught that while expression of their virility is acceptable, success in school and the workplace is a desirable means toward such expression.

Young African American males need to learn that single fatherhood detracts from rather than adds to their status. When these factors are understood and believed, virility will serve only infrequently to oppress African American female teens and change the course of the lives of African American male teen fathers for the worse.

Similarly, African American female teens should be taught how to fight sexism. They need to learn that sex is likely to lead to pregnancy and that pregnancy hurts the male's conception of them; that is, even though he often loves his child, the male teen becomes disinterested in the mother of his child. African American female teens believe that bearing a child provides a stronger tie to the father; they need to recognize that it usually leads to discontinuation of the relationship. When they thoroughly understand these matters, they can more easily choose to abstain from sex or to take every precaution not to get pregnant.

Another way to fight back at racism and sexism is for African American girls to think well of themselves regardless of their situation. No matter how deprived the circumstances, there are far better responses to racism and sexism than becoming a child-mother. When they develop such a perspective, they will have effective self-control even under circumstances apparently compelling them to be sexually active. That is, they will say no to sex and mean it or at least use contraceptives. Also, 10- to 19-year-old girls should be taught not to assume responsibility for males' desire for sex. It should be seen only as an indication that males are likely to become adult fathers. This will enable girls to shut down compelling pressure from males and their own seemingly overwhelming personal sexual desires and guilt feelings for not meeting the sexual needs of their male friends. When they can do this, they will have a more positive self-image, and young males in their teens and twenties will respect them and refrain from oppressive behaviors.

Personal love, as opposed to love for boyfriends/males, is another way to develop a positive self-image and fight sexism. So often African American girls love males more than they love themselves. One sign is that they engage in sex without contraception and directly or indirectly consent to bear children out of wedlock. They should be taught—in the home, school, religious, and community settings—to love themselves far more than they love young men. Proud love for one's self enables minority girls to say no, with self-esteem, to sex. Then they can say, with equal pride, "If you loved me, you wouldn't want me to engage in sex."

In fighting racism and sexism, minority girls should also be taught that life is difficult but that it can be made easier by cherishing one's freedom. They should learn, before puberty, the adverse consequences of sex and the life-altering effects of parenthood, along with the positive effects of virginity or safe sex.

Widespread and effective implementation of these intertwined, structural changes and personal and interpersonal behaviors could reduce minority teenage pregnancy and the impact of racism, sexism, class stratification, and low self-esteem in the American South. There seems to be no stronger linkage between societal and individual characteristics to prevent pregnancy than for racism and sexism to be eradicated and self-esteem enhanced, and for white Americans, African American males, and African American female teens to work together to prevent African American female teens from becoming mothers in the American South.

Mutual Aid Societies and Economic Development: Survival Efforts

Charles Williams, Jr., and Hilda J. B. Williams

Samuel Johnson, the eighteenth-century English author, was once asked to describe Boswell, his companion and biographer. "Boswell," he stated, "is a very clubable man." Johnson did not mean that Boswell deserved to be attacked with a club. He was referring to Boswell's fondness for all sorts of clubs and associations, a fondness he shared with many of his contemporaries. The tendency to form associations or self-help groups was not unique to eighteenth-century England. At all times and in all areas of the world, we find evidence of human beings' "clubability."

In this paper, we examine the functions and purposes of various African American self-help groups known as "mutual aid societies." Although they vary considerably, mutual aid societies exhibit several common characteristics: (1) some kind of formal, institutionalized structure; (2) the exclusion of some people; (3) members with common interests or purposes; and (4) members with a discernible sense of pride and feeling of belonging. However, mutual aid societies are not based on kinship or territory.

We contend that the activities of mutual aid among African Americans were provided to a large degree through the efforts of voluntary associations. The black church often served as the locus of control for these voluntary efforts. When viewed as activities of socioeconomic interdependence and support, mutual aid societies become functionally significant in the roles they play in a class and racially stratified society. Therefore, mutual aid societies are the primary adaptive mechanisms used by urban African Americans to cope with or adjust to new sociocultural situations. For purposes of this presentation, mutual aid societies will be treated as synonymous with voluntary associations.

The notion that mutual aid societies are a means of sociocultural adaptation is expressed by anthropologists Drake and Cayton (1945), Little (1964), Kerri (1976), and Williams and Williams (1984). Drake and Cayton viewed the high participation rate of African Americans in mutual aid efforts as "an adaptive response" to segregation (Drake and Cayton 1945:120–28). They argued that the system of segregation denied African Americans opportunities for self-expression, achievement, and self-fulfillment within the context of the larger society. Therefore, African Americans resorted to self-reliance and developed a variety of mutual aid efforts through their voluntary associations. Based upon his work in West African urban centers, Little (1964) demonstrates that voluntary associations are created by rural migrants to aid them in their adjustment to new urban situations. Lacking traditional means of support such as compact kin groups and neighbors, the new migrants addressed this deficit by forming self-help associations (Little 1964:24). Research on the black church and African Americans in the Mid-South also indicates that voluntary associations are "creative efforts of socio-cultural adaptation to a hostile environment" (Williams and Williams 1984:19). African Americans' migration patterns from the agrarian South to urban centers of the North resemble those found among Africans. African Americans faced distinctly different circumstances given the existence of the oppressive caste-like systems of both the South and the North. Regardless of the difficulties, they have managed to survive through the ingenuity, strength, and creativity of mutual aid societies.

HISTORICAL DEVELOPMENT OF MUTUAL AID SOCIETIES

In America, old myths and stereotypes die hard. One of the most pervasive myths has been the widely held view that historically African Americans have been dependent on the benevolence and generosity of white Americans for socioeconomic survival. Another supporting myth, perpetuated mainly by scholars, has been that African Americans have engaged in few, if any, self-help activities such as ethnic mutual aid societies. Several of these scholars have gone to great lengths to contrast the absence of a self-help tradition in the African American community with the extensive network of social service institutions that have served as the foundation for the economic advancement of many European ethnic groups. According to several African American scholars, including W. E. B. DuBois, E. Franklin Frazier, Carter G. Woodson (1945), and John Hope Franklin (1967), the realities of the African American experience are far different.

A critical examination of historical data suggests that mutual aid societies or self-help groups have a long and honored tradition in the African American community. Frazier (1963:26) contends that "among African Americans, as among other peoples in various parts of the world, organization for mutual aid in times of stress constituted the earliest form of social cooperation." Therefore, mutual aid traditions have been central to the development and survival of African Americans, similar to those of any other ethnic group in U.S. society. In fact, without the strong proclivity of African Americans to help themselves, it is quite doubtful that they would have survived as a distinct cultural entity in America. Frazier (1963:367) further contends that "under the slave system cooperation for mutual aid could not exist because any form of independent collective action on the part of the slaves constituted a threat to the institution of slavery."

The concept of mutual aid societies developed among the rural, free African Americans both in the North and the South immediately following Emancipation. The newly founded freedom of the slaves contributed directly to the rapid growth of mutual aid societies in the rural environment. Therefore, these rural organizations are viewed as the earliest attempts of African Americans at social and economic cooperation. Social and economic cooperation for mutual aid in times of crisis were major elements of the rural folk culture of African Americans. The primary objective of these early self-help groups was elimination of the suffering associated with sickness and death. Primarily because they developed directly from various religious organizations within the black church, they were usually sacred in nature.

Shortly after Emancipation, more formal types of mutual aid societies, such as fraternal organizations, began to flourish, particularly in the urban environment. As the rural African American became more urbanized, sacred mutual aid societies became less important and were eventually replaced by the more secular forms of organizations, such as insurance companies and fraternal organizations like the Elks, Greek letter organizations, and Prince Hall Masons. These organizations were more beneficial to the new secular status of the urban African American.

FUNCTION AND ROLE OF MUTUAL AID SOCIETIES

Anthropologists and sociologists have traditionally examined mutual aid in situations of sickness, labor exchange, and economic distress. These activities have been performed locally and very largely under such primary-group auspices as family and relatives, neighborhood groups, friendship groups, and local religious groups.

The traditionally held view of mutual aid societies was that they functioned as primary agents of social and economic development. In fact, the black church as an institution, developed directly from the efforts of mutual aid. In order to establish their own churches, African Americans throughout the North and South pooled their meager economic resources to buy buildings and the land on which they stood. At the same time, ethical and beneficial brotherhoods grew out of the churches into such groups as the Free African Society (DuBois 1899:19–20). The central point for our study is that these benevolent societies grew out of the church and were inspired by a spirit of Christian charity. The influence of the simple religious conceptions of rural African Americans and the Bible is revealed in the names of these mutual aid societies, many of which continue to exist today in the Mid-South: Love and Charity, Builders of the Walls of Jerusalem, Sons and Daughters of Esther, Brothers and Sisters of Charity, and Brothers and Sisters of Love (Raper 1926:374).

The function of mutual aid societies among African Americans extended far beyond social and economic developments. They also functioned as agencies of socialization and social control. In Memphis, organizations such as the King's Daughters, the Nineteenth Century Club, the WCA, and the Anti-Saloon League helped to spread Christian religion and education. The league's members were advised to "acquire real estate, avoid intemperance, and cultivate true manhood." Several of these societies were pivotal in the social and political reform movement launched in Memphis during the early 1900s (Harkins 1982:113). Other efforts of socialization provided by the mutual aid societies can be seen clearly in the educational development of African Americans in the Mid-South. Immediately following Emancipation and the great educational crusade carried on by northern white missionaries among the freedmen, African Americans were given a much freer hand in developing their own educational institutions. Mutual aid societies in the Mid-

South became the cornerstone of African American secondary schools, colleges, and seminaries. African American institutions such as Ownes College (currently Le Moyne Ownes College, Memphis), Lane College (Jackson, Tennessee), Rust College, and Mississippi Industrial College (both of Holly Springs, Mississippi) were developed and maintained by the mutual aid efforts of African Americans. These particular institutions were permeated with a religious and moral outlook on life. Their graduates went forth as missionaries to raise the moral and religious level of the members of their ethnic group. Many of their graduates were ministers or became ministers in these educational environments.

Another often-forgotten function of these societies was their recruitment of members of their group for political leadership. Historical literature of African Americans supports the claim that the majority of the recruited leaders were ministers. It was inevitable that ministers who had played such an important role in the organized religious life of African Americans should become political leaders during the Reconstruction period, when African Americans enjoyed some degree of civil rights.

MUTUAL AID SOCIETIES AND ROTATING
CREDIT ASSOCIATIONS

Similarities exist among different ethnic mutual aid societies, but the comparison breaks down when we examine the success rate of various ethnic groups within U.S. society. For instance, in a comparison of African Americans' mutual aid societies with rotating credit associations of other ethnic groups, we can see the advance of some ethnic groups in societies and the limited advances of others.

Geertz (1962:241–63), in his cogent analysis of rotating credit associations, reveals that "neither large-scale international capital transfers nor improvements in the terms of trade can, in themselves, bring about domestic capital accumulation in the absence of effective efforts to raise the level of domestic saving." Rotating credit associations have been created and used effectively by various ethnic groups, such as Jews and Chinese, to raise the level of their domestic saving. As defined by Geertz, rotating credit associations are usually ethnic in origin and serve the purpose of promoting individual savings, organizing them, and making them fruitful to the saver and to the community. These credit associations are adapted to different individual needs and possibilities and fitted into community patterns. Their primary goal is to encourage planned savings that benefit both the individual member and the ethnic community as a whole.

The Chinese *wui* serves as a rotating credit association of capital formation, one that is rooted in the home communities of Chinese immigrants. Only people with a relationship based upon kinship, friendship, associational connections, village mates, or classmates can be accepted into the *wui*. Members contribute a sum of money into a common pool. The highest bidder collects the pool and pays back to one member each month his contribution with interest. Thus, a member who collected the pool of $5,000 from twenty members will have to pay $250 plus interest to each of the twenty members within a period of twenty months. The *wui* was instrumental in the establishment of many Chinese businesses and persists in present-day Chinatown. In the face of past racism that precluded the Chinese from obtaining loans from financial institutions of the larger white society, saving became a habit of the Chinese immigrants. Saving efforts of the rotating credit association have propelled the Chinese into the mainstream marketplace as equal competitors. Rotating credit associations have proven beneficial for the advancement of the Chinese as an ethnic group in U.S. society.

As effective as they were, mutual aid societies stemming from the black church did not provide the same economic development for the African American community. The mutual aid efforts of African Americans have not advanced them in the marketplace for several reasons:

1. African Americans are not, nor do they see themselves as, an ethnically homogeneous group as compared to the Chinese.
2. The economic efforts of mutual aid among African Americans have been highly fragmented and geared more toward sheer survival as opposed to successful advancement.
3. Integration diminished the capacity and strength of the incidental collective actions of African Americans toward economic development.

African Americans in the United States historically have been denied basic rights of access to both institutional and environmental resources for meeting socioeconomic needs. Historically this denial has occurred at a time when other ethnic minorities and immigrant groups have utilized the voluntary sector through the formation of the rotating credit association as an adaptive mechanism for developing viable social and economic institutions.

As shown in the above examples, African Americans have had to develop their social and economic institutions under slightly different conditions, such as the risk of great danger or an atmosphere of special legislation or moral sanction, which have limited their development. Unlike some other minority groups, African Americans were not given a choice between separatism (developing institutions alien to or outside of the larger society) and integration (participating in institutions of the larger society). They either had to develop their own institutions or they had to exist without them. Despite these obstacles, African Americans have attempted for more than 360 years to neutralize and overcome hostile environmental forces imposed by the social conditions resulting from slavery, segregation, and racism in the wider society.

CONCLUSION

Contrary to the popular belief that blacks have not been involved in self-help activity, a critical review of the historical records of various mutual aid societies reveals that African Americans have pooled their resources for cooperative purposes for nearly two hundred years in both rural and urban environments.

Mutual aid societies for African Americans have historically served as vehicles to promote and support their efforts at survival in the face of adversity, particularly in the areas of economics and politics. Uniquely, while serving as a coping mechanism, these same associations functioned as change agents in preparing their members with the skills, knowledge, and resources to effectively deal with an ever-changing urban environment. In many instances, mutual aid societies in themselves were the catalyst of change, for example, the Southern Christian Leadership Conference and the black church during the civil rights movement of the 1960s. Unlike the rotating credit associations of the Chinese, mutual aid societies for African Americans were more inclusive and community-oriented, not exclusive and family controlled.

Their plight has not been easy, yet mutual aid societies exemplify the fact that African Americans are constantly assessing their position and adjusting their strategies to cope with the changing demands of their social, economic, and political environment. Even after the civil rights movement, mutual aid societies remain one of the essential mechanisms for survival among African Americans of the Mid-South.

Reproduction and Transformation of Health Praxis and Knowledge Among Southern Blacks

Carole E. Hill

While there is a continuing debate over what constitutes southern distinctiveness, it is generally agreed that several factors have contributed to the uniqueness of southern society. The factors I wish to discuss in this paper include slavery and its legacy of racism and the historical consequences of the cultural and structural disparity between whites and blacks in the reproduction and transformation of health and medicine in the American South.[1] Breeden (1988) has recently stated that the South has a long history of poor health, and that the disease patterns in the South are a powerful force that have shaped its society and culture. Drawing upon the highly respected works of Sigerist (1943), Cartwright (1972), and McNeill (1976), he argues that the reputation for poor health helped perpetuate a negative image of the South that retarded regional development by discouraging immigration and investment. The high rate of disease symbolized a region of poverty, ignorance, backwardness, and insularity. He states that "without doubt, the high incidence of disease and its effects retarded social and economic development and contributed to the national image of southern backwardness" (1988:8).

This image persists, mainly because the image is true. The South has the lowest health status in the United States. It has the second highest infant mortality rate, the most work-related medical problems, the highest rate of postnatal mortality, the lowest life expectancy, the fewest number of doctors and medical professionals per capita, a lack of adequate outpatient service and preventive care departments, and a substandard health care delivery system in rural areas. Now, as has been true in the past, minority groups and the poor are the least healthy of all southerners (Breeden 1988).

To understand and explain this historical pattern, it is necessary to look beyond the regional to the local level, on the one hand, and, on the other, to the world system. Within this complex system, I will single out blacks in the American South, particularly in Georgia, in an attempt to explain how the peculiar configuration of race and class in the region continues to reproduce and transform itself within the context of the power, knowledge, and practice of Western medicine.

THE MEASURES OF WELLNESS

On the basis of the generally accepted measures of wellness, whites in the South are healthier and blacks sicker. This disparity is a historical fact, with programs to improve health being targeted at generalized groups (such as the poor or mothers and children) rather than toward blacks. Furthermore, the overall economic and social differences are not usually addressed in health policies. The unique position of blacks in southern society (their culture and structure) and the nature of the linkages (social, economic, and political) to complex systems of which they are a part, result in inequities in black health care. Jones and Rice (1987) argue that there are three major explanations of the health conditions among blacks in the United States. They are: (1) institutionalized racism, (2) economic inequality, and (3) access barriers. Each assumes race as the primary factor for the distribution of health care services. I would add class as a factor, as well, in explaining not only the level of wellness but, in addition, the responses blacks have to the health care system. Before examining these factors within the complex systems of health care, I will review the results of racism and classism through measures of wellness.

Health status is usually measured by fertility, mortality, and life expectancy. While fertility in American women has been declining in the past four decades (from 1950 to 1980, the crude birth rate decreased by 33 percent and the fertility rate decreased by 32 percent), the birth rate for black women has remained greater than for white women. In 1980 the birth rate for black teenagers 15 to 17 years of age was about three times that of white teenagers in the same age group. For those 18 to 19, the rate was almost double.

Neonatal deaths (mortality for infants under 28 days of age) accounts for the majority of infant deaths. Data from 1980 indicate that the gap between blacks and whites on this measure has widened in the past fifty years; the neonatal rate is almost twice as high for blacks (a major factor being low birth weight). A similar trend can be seen for maternal mortality. The difference in rates for blacks increased from 2.4 times as high in 1940 to 3.2 times as high in 1980. Lack of prenatal care remains a major problem for black women. According to a 1989 U.S. government report, 39 percent of black women received no prenatal care in the first trimester, compared to 21 percent of white women. For blacks, the infant mortality rate is 17.9, compared to 8.6 for white babies (ranking the United States worst among the industrialized nations in infant mortality). From 1920 to 1980, there has been a significant increase in life expectancy for both blacks and whites. The racial differentiation declined from 9.6 percent to 4.9 percent overall with a very small shift for black males as compared to white males. Life expectancy for black men has declined to 65.1 years, compared to 75.6 years for white men (National Center for Health Statistics 1990).

Mortality rates, in addition, continue to demonstrate a disparity between the two races. The leading U.S. cause of death stems from diseases of the heart. The mortality rate from coronary heart disease is almost 50 percent higher for black males than white males. Although mortality rates in general have been declining for this category, the percentage difference between black and white males has been increasing, while those for women has shown a decline. Likewise, death from cancer, the second leading cause of death in the United States, illustrates the same trend—from 1960 to 1980, the age-adjusted cancer mortality rate increased 28 percent for white men and 82 percent for black men. For females, there was a decline of 2 percent for blacks and 10 percent for whites.

The third leading cause of death in the United States is cerebrovascular disease (stroke). Since 1960 the rates have been decreasing for both blacks and whites. Similar to other trends, we find a slight increase in the percentage difference among black men compared to white men. Contrarily, the black female percentage difference has been declining. Death from accidents and other adverse effects is the fourth leading cause of death in the United States and is the leading cause of death for persons 1 to 34 years of age. Motor vehicle accidents, which account for 50 percent of the deaths in these categories, were 31 percent higher for black males than for white males and 17 percent higher for black females than black males in 1980.

Again, obvious disparities exist between blacks and whites for the fifth, sixth, and seventh leading causes of death. Pneumonia and influenza had a 72 percent difference in mortality between black and white females, while the difference between these two populations for diabetes mellitus increased 40 percent from 1960 to 1980, to a rate of 86 percent higher for blacks. For chronic liver disease and cirrhosis, in 1960 the difference was negligible (2.8 percent), but by 1980, the difference in mortality had risen to 94 percent with the mortality rate for black males increasing 200 percent and 35 percent for white females. Lastly, U.S. data indicate that mortality from homicides and legal intervention is seven times higher for black males than for white males, with a 60 percent increase in mortality since 1970 for black males and a 36 percent increase for white males (Rene 1987).

How does this epidemiological data for the United States compare to statistics in the South? For purposes of illustration and because all my fieldwork in the South has been in Georgia, I will present similar data from that state. In 1988, the crude birth rate for Georgia was 16.7 per thousand females aged 15 to 44. The white rate was 14.5 and the black rate 21.8. From 1975 to 1985 the infant mortality rate in Georgia declined from 18.3 per thousand live births to 12.7. The 1988 rate was 12.5. When the races are compared, however, we find the same pattern as in the nation; in 1988, the white rate was 9 infant deaths per thousand, while the black rate was 19.5 infant deaths per thousand, more than double. Indeed, Georgia ranks forty-eighth or forty-ninth each year in infant mortality, placing behind Washington, D.C., Mississippi, and South Carolina. Forty percent of these deaths were in urban areas and 60 percent in rural areas. Seventy percent of all infant deaths are due to low birth weight babies.

Cardiovascular mortality ranks as the major cause of death in Georgia. The same differential patterns between races exist in Georgia as in the U.S. data. The rates for blacks are significantly higher than for whites. With age-adjusted rates, the differentials are just as evident, as we can see with the rates for acute myocardial infarction. The second cause of mortality in Georgia is cancer. Again, we can see that the gap appears to be widening among black and white males and narrowing somewhat among black and white females in the decade between 1975 and 1985.

The third cause of death in Georgia is cerebrovascular disease, with a significant disparity between races, reflecting a widening of the gap in wellness, especially in comparing black men to white men. Violent deaths from accidents follows the U.S. pattern as the fourth major cause of mortality in Georgia. While rates indicate that more whites are killed in motor vehicle accidents, the age-adjusted rates show that after 30 years of age a larger percentage of black males are killed than white males, while the lower rates for black females remains throughout all ages. Similar patterns exist for all other accidents. The fifth and sixth causes of death in Georgia are influenza and pneumonia, and diseases of the arteries and capillaries. The rates for both these diseases again illustrate a large differential between the races, as do the rates for diabetes and cirrhosis.

These epidemiological data conclusively demonstrate that the wellness gap between blacks and whites is significant and appalling (Amler and Dull 1987; U.S. Department of Health and Human Services 1985, 1986; National Center for Health Statistics 1990). The growing gap in life expectancies for blacks and whites is due almost entirely to deaths from causes such as AIDS, drug abuse, alcoholism, and car accidents and not to diseases such as heart disease, cancer, and stroke. It has widened, however, from 1984 to 1987 (Hilts 1989).

Historically, the life expectancy gap had been narrowing since 1900 (when statistics were first compiled) until 1984, when it began to widen, which, more or less, corresponds with a widening gap in many of the major causes of mortality. What has happened in the past decade to foster the wellness of whites over blacks, and does this trend reflect an overall cultural and structural pattern in southern society that is being reproduced rather than transformed in the health arena? To answer these questions, and in an attempt to find meaning in the statistical data, we need to look at how this population links to and interacts with the culture and structure of larger systems and how the larger political economy links to and interacts with the black population within the context of health and illness. We know that more blacks are in poverty and increasingly are falling into severe poverty. For example, in 1978, one third of poor blacks had an income of less than $5,000 a year (a family of three is poor if its annual income is less than $10,000). In 1987 almost half of poor blacks earned below $5,000 in Georgia (Georgia Department of Human Resources 1987).

STRUCTURAL REPRODUCTION AND TRANSFORMATION

"In our time," said Thomas Mann, "the destiny of man presents its meaning in political terms" (quoted in Gordiner 1989). In a capitalistic system, the distribution of power, knowledge, and wealth are unevenly distributed. Southern society is historically based on an agrarian economic model that rewarded the large landowners and created what Warner and Davis (1939) and Dollard (1937) called a "color caste" system. Within each caste existed a class system. These biases and prejudices were reflected in blacks' inability to take advantage of the economic and political opportunities of the larger systems or, stated another way, classism and racism have been barriers to their economic and political power and, consequently, to their quality of life and health status in comparison to the more powerful racial and class groups. Drake (1965) characterizes this situation as "victimization" of blacks since the social system operates in a way as to deprive them of a chance to share in the more desirable material and nonmaterial products of a society that is dependent, in part, upon their labor and loyalty. Blacks have not had the same degree of access to money, contacts, education, and "know-how" (1965:772). Using two concepts developed by Max Weber, life chances and life styles, Drake explains that direct victimization occurs when people are denied access to economic and political power and indirect victimization is found in the consequences that flow from a social structure that decreases life chances, consequences such as high morbidity and mortality rates, low longevity rates, and reduced life-styles. This framework was used by Weber to compare individuals and groups with respect to those ways of behaving that vary in the amount of esteem, honor, and prestige attached to them. Differences in "life chances" may make it impossible to acquire the money or education (or limit contacts) necessary for adopting and maintaining prestigious life styles. Drake feels that because blacks have different life styles, white society segregates them—it institutionalizes racism and classism.

Linkages to the Health System

A complex systems model (Hill 1988) assumes that health systems (including the medical system) are part of a large social system. It is important to analyze how the components of the micro- and macrolevels of the systems connect; the microlevel is the people who make up a family, household, community—locally based structures and cultures. The macro is the people who develop and implement health policies and programs framed within a particular structure and culture. Linkages of people, of structure, of cultures at the various levels of the system interact in a multidimensional hierarchy. Many of these linkages are ambiguous and replete with discontinuities and contradictions. One reality permeates them—maldistribution of power, knowledge, equality, and justice (Wolf 1982, Mintz 1977, Silverman 1979, and Trouillot 1984). It is in the negotiation process among the levels that reproduction and transformations take place in the levels of the complex systems. This approach is energized by *critiquing* the nature of the linkages among the hierarchical levels of the health systems. As information is obtained as to how and why the levels create, break, or maintain links, statements can be made about the reproduction and transformation of the structures and cultures of the people who are making the complex systems of health and the degree of domination/subordination and resistance.

There are several structural factors that guide the nature of interaction between the dominant medical system and the black population. One frequently used measure is utilization of medical services, broken down into several medical service categories such as ambulatory care, inpatient care, and extended care. Another measure includes the distribution of health care services (availability and access) with a third measure—the amount of money spent on health care services by populations—generally broken down by income, age, sex, and region of the country.

Historically, blacks have been structured out of the dominant medical system. Savitt (1988) informs us that during the time of slavery, whites were required by law to provide medical care to slaves, who by 1860 numbered four million. Although many whites believed that blacks were medically different from whites, medical services provided to blacks were, of course, based upon their European experiences. The white master or overseer would first use home remedies and only call a physician if they did not seem to work. They would often call "irregular practitioners," such as homeopaths and hydropaths, reflecting their own assumptions about black health. Black women were frequently "trusted" to provide health services to slaves by administering traditional remedies of blacks combined with some white remedies. And, especially in rural areas, prenatal and obstetrical care (midwifery) was performed by black women (often to whites).

While some merging took place, blacks for the most part used their traditional health system to treat illnesses and were reluctant to use the white system and medicine. According to Savitt (1988), slaves preferred their own medicine, herbs, and root doctors or conjurers, and frequently would not report illnesses to their white masters until they had reached a serious stage and consequently required more extensive medical care. Free blacks, who composed about 10 percent of the antebellum black population, were worse off than slaves. They were "at the bottom of the health care hierarchy" (Savitt 1978:217).

Blacks have continued to hold these positions in the hierarchy of the complex system to the present day. After Emancipation, a pattern of discrimination against blacks was set in motion, due mainly to (1) beliefs that blacks were inferior and different from whites and that they had different diseases and (2) their "victimization" in the social system. These themes persisted until the civil rights movement. After the civil rights movement, Medicaid (enacted in 1966) was established to provide medical services to the poor and especially to blacks. At this point, utilization rates increased as blacks were more formally associated with the dominant system. This increased interaction brought about by more formal linkages began to increase their awareness of the medical system, which in turn began to impact their health beliefs, a subject to be discussed in the next section.

In the United States, the number of physician visits per person remained relatively constant up to 1980, with older and younger people and women of child-bearing age using more services. In 1964, the poor had fewer visits than the nonpoor, but by 1975 the situation had reversed. Not only did the poor use medical services more, but there was an increase in hospital emergency room use by blacks compared to whites. Furthermore, from 1964 to 1980, there was a decrease in utilization of physicians for people earning over $25,000, while those earning under $7,000 increased their visits. A greater number of whites visited a physician in his or her office rather than in a clinic or hospital. In the South, physician visits increased from 4.3 to 4.6 per person from 1964 to 1980, with utilization by blacks increasing more than whites. Similar trends are found in black hospital outpatient visits, while whites utilized the doctor's office more frequently. While blacks are utilizing medical services more frequently, they are waiting longer to do so and, consequently, have longer stays in hospitals (an average of two days longer than whites). Similar patterns exist for admissions to mental health facilities.

The financing of medical services has changed over the past two and one-half decades with the creation of Medicare and Medicaid. In 1950 two-thirds of personal medical costs were paid by patients. In 1975 two-thirds were paid by third parties, and by 1981 67.9 percent were paid by third parties. The cost for these payments has dramatically increased over the past decade, particularly payments to physicians.

Persons with Medicaid had the lowest out-of-pocket expenses in 1980. Medicaid is financed jointly by federal and state funds, but it is administered independently by each state with broad federal guidelines. Thus, each state determines eligibility, duration of coverage, and methods and levels of reimbursement. In 1989 Georgia increased Medicaid coverage to pregnant women and infants at 100 percent of poverty level for the purpose of extended medical care. It is currently 133 percent of poverty level. As stated earlier, the populations that are increasing more rapidly are children and single mothers. (The number of children living in poverty has increased in recent years, with less than 4 percent of them covered by Medicaid.) One of the reasons for this situation is that thirty states (all the southern states) do not offer Medicaid to families that are considered to live intact, even though family income is low enough to qualify for aid. Furthermore, no state provides coverage for individuals up to the poverty level, and in twenty-nine states (all the southern states included), the limit for Medicaid is less than 50 percent of the federal poverty level. An increase in minimum wage, which renders many poor blacks ineligible for food stamps, recently has complicated the situation.

Statistics comparing the financing of medical services are not broken down by region. Comparing blacks and whites nationally, however, we find that in 1980 Medicaid covered 15.5 percent of the white population and 12.9 percent of the black population, while Medicare covered 6.2 percent of whites and 24.2 percent of blacks. It covered 65.1 percent of poor blacks and 30.9 percent of poor whites. Among the near poor, 14.7 percent of whites and 25.1 percent of blacks were covered (U.S. Department of Health and Human Resources 1985). It should be noted that many doctors do not accept Medicaid payments. In Georgia, a Medicaid-eligible woman, for example, must find a doctor who is willing to accept this form of payment. Physicians can make more money by taking patients with other forms of third-party payments or out-of-pocket payments. Also, many physicians are concerned about malpractice lawsuits. Their risks are increased by serving high-risk women. The percentage of people under 65 years not covered by health insurance is very high in the South. In Georgia 18 percent of the population are without coverage of any kind, making it extremely difficult for almost 20 percent of the population.

The problem is particularly apparent in the areas of child care, maternal care, and life expectancy. Many women cannot obtain prenatal care, which often results in higher infant mortality rates. For example, Clay County is the poorest county in Georgia, with over 40 percent of its population living in poverty. Its infant mortality rate is twice that of the state's average, and its average life expectancy is 65.3 years. In 1985 it budgeted $8.67 per citizen for public health expenditures (Hine 1987). The United States spent $1,926 per person on medical care in 1986—which leads the world in spending, even though its life expectancy dropped from fifteenth to seventeenth in the past five years.

A recent anthropological study attempted to delineate reasons for an infant mortality rate of 12.8 in the Georgia county, which stood adjacent to another county with a rate of 9.5. It concentrated on the structural situation and behavior of thirty-three black pregnant women. It found them to be young, poor, unemployed, undereducated, and financially dependent (mostly on their mothers, sisters, or fathers). They had inadequate diets and were protein deficient, all used caffeine, and more than half smoked cigarettes on a daily basis. Only eight had access to health insurance, and they used medical service infrequently. Only one had a regular physician, and three had seen a pediatrician for their children. Transportation was not a problem; rather, money was the major barrier to medical care. Most did not have a clear understanding of the services that were available to them in the county, and they did not know how to use the system. They wanted to use a hospital for the delivery of their babies. Physicians began to require that women obtain prenatal care

from them rather than from the county health department if they delivered their babies in a hospital. This precluded them from having either
prenatal care or delivery in a hospital. In addition, physicians resisted
accepting Medicaid. The adjacent county is one of the more affluent
counties in the state, with a high educational level and with a very successful midwifery program, factors that account for the difference in
infant mortality rates (Blisset 1987).

Services available to indigent pregnant women in Georgia vary widely
from county to county. There are sixty-nine counties in Georgia that
have no obstetrician/gynecologists or general practitioners. There are
no state or federal monies available for physicians, nurse-midwives, or
deliveries for normal, healthy non–Medicaid-eligible women who cannot find a physician. Seventeen counties offer no prenatal care other than
Women, Infants and Children (WIC) Screening. Thirty-one of Georgia's 159 counties have no hospitals, and twenty-one hospitals have no
obstetric services, while sixty-seven counties are without a physician
available to deliver babies. In 1984 Georgia implemented a law that
stated that no hospital offering emergency service can refuse aid to any
woman in active labor, and that the woman's county of residence is responsible for reimbursing the hospital for its services. It did not provide
for state-level funding.

While traditional health behavioral patterns, such as midwifery, are
often suggested as means to increase the wellness of the poor and blacks,
many are generally opposed by the dominant medical groups who primarily control the policies in the country, region, and state. Tinkering
with the system has produced dynamics without change. While more
people have been linked to the medical system, within the past decade
the health status of blacks has not been enhanced. In the South they
remain poorer and in worse health than people in all other regions in the
United States. Basically, the medical system has been reproducing its
structure, thereby bringing benefits to the same powerful interest groups
at the expense of effective linkages for minorities. In this process of the
social construction of racism, blacks continue to be "victimized."

CULTURAL REPRODUCTION AND TRANSFORMATION

While the culture at the macrolevel of the groups that make policies and plan change has been implicitly mentioned in the previous paragraphs, in this section I will discuss the culture of the people on the local level by drawing on the findings of my research among blacks in Coberly, a small rural community in Georgia. I will discuss these people, their culture, and the behavior that results from the dialectic stress between their culture and the surrounding structure.[2] Blacks make up 47 percent of the population of Coberly.[3] They are a poor, structured minority, deprived of the basic necessities of health care that are available to the majority of the dominant class.

Culture provides the various subgroups that participate in the health systems with ways of making sense of the unpredictability of life experiences, with means for setting goals and for guiding behavior by providing rules and symbols that help them understand and explain, but not necessarily accept, their structured position. Culture provides the avenues for overcoming the paradoxes of life; it provides an order that makes sense of the world that people construct in times of wellness, illness, and suffering. It is through human actions and their meanings that systems are reproduced and transformed on all levels.

Wellness and illness are experiential. They are evaluated as positive or negative depending upon the beliefs, values, life experiences, and the linkages that individuals and groups have in the systems that determine their opportunity. These cultural and structural parameters create internal and external constraints on health behavior. Is medical care a right or a privilege? Who is most responsible for a person's health? The answers to such questions are cultural as well as political in that they are based upon how groups or individuals experience alternative health systems and on their position in the structure of the whole social system. Therefore, in southern society poor blacks, because of their structure, have a finite set of options to relieve sickness and suffering and obtain wellness. These options are not arbitrarily chosen. The social, economic, and political structure defines their possibilities and opportunities and delimits the linkages they can make to the culture and structure of the dominant medical system in the larger society.

Culture limits the range of illness and wellness behaviors blacks can choose. What behaviors become meaningful to black southerners are, in part, based on *their* history and culture and, in part, based on their structural position in the dominant culture. The threads of the past are linked to ever changing present experience. While enduring racism and classism, black southerners are also actors who make decisions that constitute their own culture and structure within that of the dominant culture and structure.

Black southerners, like every other population, believe in and use several health systems that represent strategies for survival within the context of racism. Stack (1974) described similar survival techniques in a black community in a midwestern city. The people of Coberly frequently use a wide variety of self-help remedies such as herbs, over-the-counter medicines, spiritual healers, root doctors, conjurers, and other religious practitioners. These traditional health systems are utilized along with a physician, when possible, to insure health (preventive medicine) and to heal illnesses (curative medicine).

There are some illnesses and situations that can only be helped by physicians and others that require another kind of healer. Thus, physicians are just one resource for these blacks in maintaining their wellness and treating their illnesses. Consequently, when a new health facility is opened or a new program is initiated from the macrolevel, it is often viewed as just another option, which may or may not be utilized. Utilization depends on the cultural and structural linkages to the dominant system related to the kinds of services rendered. If people opt not to use a new clinic or service (as is happening now in an inner city health clinic in Atlanta), then we have dynamics without change. No transformation takes place. Although the idea of a new clinic was culturally meaningful to the policymakers and health planners, it did not "fit" the culture of the target population, who had no input into the planning and implementation of the clinic. Thus, a clash of meanings, of texts, occurred— an access problem not in terms of economics or distance but of cultural access.

The appropriate question is not: Do the people have access to the clinic? Rather, does the clinic have access to the people? To more clearly illustrate cultural linkages in complex systems of health, I will describe black experiences with health systems. When we shift from the limited categories of epidemiology, making blacks the object of study through using aggregate data and neglecting the cultural context of health, the data are often criticized as being nonrepresentative. Fluid and broad categories of people as subjects reveal knowledge and resources that, while being used to create meaning in a similar fashion as all humans, differ from that of peoples situated differently in a complex social system.

The People's Spaces, Illnesses, and Voices

In a complex systems model, the local level includes the culture and structure of people who for the most part become the object of health care policies and programs or the subject of statistics, but who are rarely given a voice. This is the gift anthropology gives to complex systems. Peoples' voices are heard. They become the subject. Only then can they be understood within their own cultural and structural framework as active participants, active partners in health systems. For the purposes of this paper, I will briefly describe the people of Coberly and then include a brief case study of one resident.

Coberly is a typical rural southern town whose people, both black and white, for the most part conform to the traditional plantation model in southern society, with blacks de facto segregated from whites. Its population of one thousand is gradually growing due mostly to "outsiders" moving in and purchasing land. Approximately 47 percent are black, and, in keeping with the traditional southern patterns, most live in separate sections of town, apart from whites. Most of the people had ties to the land in the past, that is, they were farmers, sharecroppers, or, in the case of some whites, owners of large tracts of land. In recent years, however, both rich and poor make a living in either small industries, services, or professional endeavors.

The majority of the people are poor. Twenty-seven percent live below the poverty line. They have a median of 8.8 years of schooling completed, with a 6 percent dropout rate and a median income of $6,652. Twelve percent of the population make over $15,000. The unemployment rate is 10 percent, and a large number of people are dependent upon governmental subsidies. There are ten churches in the town— Baptist, Methodist, and Holiness. The indicators of health status reflect those of the state. Blacks have a life expectancy of 61 years, compared to 72.6 for whites. The infant mortality rate for blacks in 1980 was 70 per thousand and in 1988 was 60 per thousand; whites compare at 0 per thousand in 1980 and 0 per thousand in 1988. While these figures are misleading due to the low numbers of births, the disparity is consistent through time.

While some blacks work for governmental service agencies, most are wage laborers in small industries. They live in two distinct neighborhoods. One is the old established one dating back to the last century. The other is newer, rather disjointed, with a mixture of blacks and whites. The older one displays a cohesion based on family ties with a lot of visiting and mutual support economically, socially, emotionally. There are no businesses in the neighborhood except for a former general store that is now a small billiard room with three or four playing tables; the proprietor sells cold drinks and snack foods. A church is located at the edge of the neighborhood.

The income spread of the sampled households ranges from $1,000 to $15,000, with most between $6,000 to $8,000. They include cleaning workers, maintenance workers, construction workers, cooks for a business and an institution, a school bus driver, a caretaker of children and retarded adults, elementary school teachers, mechanics, and various production-line workers in a textile mill and the small clothing manufacturing plant.

During the research, I observed a variety of structural arrangements in the households; the nuclear family is uncommon. For example, an older retired couple had their foster daughter and her two young children living with them. They referred to her as their daughter at first. However, when we came to the prenatal section of the interview schedule, they said she was their adopted daughter and that they had not had children themselves. After that, they said that they had never actually adopted her. Because of this, her mother had once been able to come and take her away from them. The mother, who lived in a city about seventy-five miles away at the time, abused the girl emotionally and physically. She ran away from her mother and somehow made her way back to this couple. The girl later married and moved to Texas. Recently she separated from her husband and came back to Coberly with her children to live with her "parents." An elderly brother of one of the couple had lived there until recently, when he was taken to a nursing home because he became too ill to be cared for at home. Later, there was a black wreath on their door; the brother had died. The couple also "keeps an eye out" for an elderly, deaf cousin who lives across the street. His children all live out of state. They take him to his doctor for frequent checkups and when he is sick, and they do other errands for him.

Family and neighborhood support these people. For example, when a widower in his nineties had a leg amputated, his children got together and decided that someone had to move in to care for him. It was agreed that a daughter, who is divorced with no children at home, would quit her job and care for him. The other children and some grandchildren provide them with financial support. Moreover, the support provided by the family is not purely economic. All of the houses on the short road where the man lives belong to his daughters and their husbands, and one of his granddaughters lives next door to him with her husband and two children. Everyone pitches in to share yard work and cleaning and maintenance chores. Other family members, who do not live on the same road, come often to visit and bring them things. From conversations at different times with several of the family members, it became evident that they are extremely proud of him for the kind of father and husband he has been over the years. They do not think of him as a burden or a drain on family resources. According to them, he is an asset to the family that they are lucky to have. The family collectively gives economic, social, emotional, and caretaking support to him.

Residents who leave the neighborhood often feel responsibility for their kinspeople or fictive kinspeople. For example, a man in his seventies lives alone because his wife is dead and all of his children live in Ohio or Michigan now. The children have tried to persuade him to live with one of them, but he doesn't want to leave his home or give up his independence. Other family members who live in the neighborhood, along with his neighbors, watch out for him every day. Since he is always active, if he's not seen working in his field behind the house or tinkering around the shed in his yard, someone goes over to check on him. When he is sick or has an accident, one of the neighbors, a family member, or his doctor calls his children, who keep in contact regularly in any case. If the situation (which is evaluated by the doctor) is serious enough, one of the children takes him to live with him or her while he is being treated and is recovering. Then, when he is well again, one of them brings him back home. The son, who told of several such episodes, did so matter-of-factly. Although other family members in the neighborhood could have cared for the man, his children want the responsibility of caring for him when he is incapacitated. It is obvious that the people in this neighborhood, the oldest area in the town, have strong ties and feel as though this area is "their community." These ties and feelings do not extend to the other black neighborhood previously mentioned; it is referred to as "the people from the other side of town," and derogatory statements such as "they drink too much" or "the kids do dope" or "those folks carry on" are made about it.

There is a sense of shared history and values in the neighborhood. Most people attend church regularly and feel that religion is very important in their lives. Next to the family, the church is their most important support system. The activities of the church create a social and symbolic system that functions as a resource for their survival. People talk about their trust in God, and their religious beliefs are inextricably bound to their health beliefs and behavior, as are those of many whites. They talk a lot about their "Lord Jesus Christ" and how he came to earth for their benefit. If they just follow his word, they feel, then a better life will be theirs. "The family of the Lord" is an important metaphor for these people, and they attempt to apply it to their daily lives. It is such religious symbols, combined with their sense of family and kinship, that provide the basis for the meaning these Coberly residents give to everyday life. They provide most blacks of Coberly with meaning and structure in their lives as they continue to struggle with institutionalized racism in their community, state, and region.

Health Knowledge and Behavior Linkages

Seventy percent of the blacks sampled (in thirty-four households representing 45.7 percent of the complete sample of the community) experience problems with their heart or blood. Most described these problems with the term "high blood" and said that they were aware of this illness only because the doctor or nurse had tested them when they had been seeking care for another problem. Although their doctor had told them that hypertension is serious, they believed that the doctor and his medicines would help very little; after all, the disease has no symptoms. Very few experienced problems with low blood pressure, or "low blood." Several women, however, believed that their blood has been low since miscarriages or since their "woman's operation."

Diabetes, cognitively related to "blood problems," was reported often (by 31 percent of the sample). Too much sugar in the blood is felt to run in the family. Diabetes is often self-diagnosed and treated with popular medicines until an acute episode occurs. At that time, the individual is taken to a physician for diagnosis. Several people said that they had probably suffered from sugar problems for years before a doctor diagnosed it. Many blacks interviewed expect to have diabetes, especially if they have a relative with the disease. If they perceive that the symptoms occur, they will self-treat them long before it is spotted as a health problem by medical personnel.

Over 60 percent reported arthritis and rheumatism problems, the majority of which are self-diagnosed. These disorders are viewed as very similar, often lumped together in conversation. Both bring about pain in the bones and joints and are treated similarly. Many blacks are unable to work full days or even full time because of periodic arthritic episodes. Like blood problems and diabetes, arthritis and rheumatism are accepted as a normal part of their daily lives, and adjustments to these illnesses are made as a matter of course. Similar attitudes were found with regard to some more mundane ailments, such as headaches and backaches, although very few said that these problems kept them from normal daily activities. They feel that frequent headaches (which 92 percent of respondents reported) are related to arthritis, nerves, tension, and stress, as are general aches and pains. In fact, all these illness episodes are clustered together in the minds of the blacks of Coberly.

Likewise, stomach problems are often related to nerves, tension, and stress; ulcers, on the other hand, are more frequently connected with dietary behavior than with stress. Kidney-bladder difficulties are almost always related to stomach problems. Only a few self-diagnose their stomach or kidney-bladder problems. These problems, believed to be inherited or to "run in the family," are often verbally described by relating stories about the episodes suffered by their parents, uncles and aunts, or grandparents. If the pain becomes too severe, a physician is consulted to confirm a person's diagnosis and to give him or her a shot or pill to relieve the pain.

Another kind of acute illness episode, which at times incapacitates the victim, is accidents (30 percent of those interviewed). These are mostly work-related. A majority of blacks (both male and female) work manual jobs with a high risk of accidents. If one occurs, it often causes them to miss work for days or even weeks. Furthermore, these accidents often create chronic health problems, such as arthritis.

Surgery, another illness episode that creates financial hardship, was reported only twice for black males (for a hernia and a kidney stone) and eight times for women, all related to "female problems." Fully 35 percent of the women had undergone hysterectomies, a term several of the women did not know, reporting it as a "female operation." Some reported that their doctors had told them that they should have the "female operation" for general health purposes.

Other illness episodes experienced in black households are menstrual problems, liver disorders, lung-respiratory diseases, and cancer. We had no cases of sickle cell anemia in our sample. This does not necessarily mean that these households do not suffer from this or still other health problems. They just did not report them or talk about them. Those illnesses which they did discuss were overwhelmingly described with phrases or terms like "high blood," "feeling low," "nerves," "arthritis/rheumatism," "accidents," and "headaches." Such terms form "core symbols" (Good 1977) for categorizing and explaining illnesses. These, then, are the illnesses blacks live with daily, those which have become a part of their lives.

Many people did not know the scientific terms for their illnesses and immediately translated a physician's words into their traditional categories, which have a mixed traditional-scientific etiology. In our interviews, the same process took place. We had to translate the medical terms we used into descriptive terms that were familiar to our interviewees. In their discussions of illness, they used only a few categories to describe their symptoms. Therefore, it would appear to an outsider either that they do not have certain illnesses or that they are ignorant of illnesses. These encounters made it clear to me that the nature of a physician or other health care specialist's interaction with these patients is crucial, not only for correct diagnosis of an illness, but also for making accurate assessments of the incidence of disease in rural areas. Communication along these linkage lines from people within the system consequently affects both health services and health behavior.

The Case of Helen

Helen[4] is a 28-year-old black woman who is head of a household consisting also of her 14-year-old daughter, two sons (aged 12 and 10) and her 9-month-old daughter. Another child died just after delivery.

Helen works at a local factory as a secretary. She learned to type in high school and took a six-week course at a nearby junior college. At that time her mother was living and helped take care of the children Helen had as an adolescent. Helen first became pregnant at the age of 14 because she "didn't know what she was doing." All she wanted at the time was attention from a man, to feel like a woman, and to do what she thought would keep him. She knew that her mother would take care of her and her child so that she could finish school. By the time she reached the eleventh grade, she had two children and decided to drop out and work. When she first became pregnant (she knew because she "missed two months"), she told her mother and grandmother. They were supportive and helped her as much as they could through the pregnancy (and through the other three). They gave her teas to drink regularly and would recommend "over-the-counter" medicines for any problems she encountered. She went to the public health clinic once to see what they had to say about pregnancy but was "lectured" by the nurse, so she decided not to go again. "Anyway, Mama knows more, and all they talked about was eating habits. Not to eat this and that and not to gain weight. I believe that doesn't matter. God gave me the baby, and he wants it to be healthy, not starved to death. My family knows best."

Not only did Helen not comply with the advice of the public health nurse about her first child, she didn't comply with her advice about the second either. She delivered the first child at home with a midwife attending to the birth; her family did not have enough money to pay a doctor or the hospital. For the third and fourth child, they saved the money and borrowed some from relatives. Toward the end of each of these pregnancies, Helen went to see the doctor who would deliver her babies. Her experience with the second child became one of those "certain circumstances" in which she thought that "the doctor knows best." She had some trouble with the pregnancy, so she consulted a doctor in the eighth month; he told her she might lose the baby. At that point, she complied with his prescriptions and "tried to do what he said." She took the medicines along with the teas and herbs given her by her grandmother. She also prayed to God and began to "look to him for guidance." Today, she thinks that God helped her much more than the doctor, who only cost her money. In fact, it was always difficult to find doctors who would deliver the babies; Helen had to prove to them that she had the money to pay before they would consent to have her admitted into the hospital to deliver a baby. The second baby died three days after birth. So, during the subsequent two pregnancies, she consulted a doctor earlier. She still did not comply with all the dieting advice or take all the medicines he prescribed. However, "they came out all right." The doctor gave her pills to take after every meal. Helen is still confused about how often he meant. She eats only two meals a day and wonders if he meant three times a day.

Another "certain circumstance" in which Helen complied with the prescription of the medical system was when her mother had cancer.

> We knew something was wrong long before the doctor found out what it was. She was losing weight and feeling real bad all the time. The teas didn't do any good or the medicines the man up there in Magnolia told her to take. We knew that she needed those tests the doctor gives in his office and finally they told [the doctor] what was wrong. She had cancer in her lower intestines. She was operated on and when she came home, she recovered enough to get around the house. At first, she had to go for those cobalt treatments that made her sick. She didn't want to go, but I made her. I thought they would help. She took most of the medicine the doctor gave her and drank special teas everyday. She really thought that only God could save her.

Two years after her operation, Helen's mother became severely ill and died. Helen thinks that the doctors did all they could, they just didn't know enough to save her. Like most people in Coberly, Helen makes her own decisions about how and when and from whom to seek health care and the degree to which she accepts their treatments.

Compliance with the prescriptions of the medical system involves a complex set of behaviors and beliefs, which was illustrated in the cultural models of the people of Coberly. Such models are different for different subpopulations, and their illness experiences expand in response to illness. Compliance is a matter of degree; it depends upon the individual's cultural, social, and economic circumstances. Variability in compliance, therefore, is not surprising among blacks in Coberly.

Linkage Resistance and Compliance

People link to "the system" (Ortner 1984) in particular ways and, at the same time, the system links to them in particular ways. The uniqueness of the linkages depend on (1) the culture and structure of the

particular part of the complex system (in this case medical system) and
(2) the culture and structure of the targeted group (in this case, blacks).
Cultural linkages are less obvious and more difficult to construct since
they are not measured by numbers but words, beliefs, symbols, meanings, and behaviors that are not often measured or considered important
by the dominant group. They have to be delineated through systematically measuring and experiencing what people say, how they behave,
what they believe, and the patterns that are derived from these words
and observations.

In Coberly, blacks experience illness differently from whites, and
their behavior depends on the internal and external constraints of racism.
Their illness episodes and response to illnesses reflect their status in the
social structures. Their history and their experience and knowledge tells
them which health system to link into first; which resources to utilize.
These judgments and the associated behavior—just like those for preventive health or health seeking behavior—are the basis on which to
find their linkages (active decision making) and the convergences and
divergences with the dominant culture.

In Coberly, I found differences between blacks and whites in the
meaning and interpretations of symptoms and subsequent behavior.
Knowledge of symptoms, illnesses, and diseases not only differed between blacks and whites but also between the medical system categories. Blacks reported half as many symptoms as whites as the basis for
seeking a physician, and they discussed multiple symptoms more frequently before deciding to visit a physician. They waited longer periods
of time before contacting a medical facility. Whites discussed a variety
of options, but mostly within the medical domain, while blacks re-
counted more options that link to health systems other than the medical
one. Whites used the medical system more often for chronic illnesses,
and the utilization rate was similar in acute illnesses. In terms of preventive health behavior, whites used the available medical options (that is,
check-ups, screenings, Pap tests, high blood pressure tests) more than
blacks, with the exception of blood pressure checks. Blacks, as well as
poorer whites, rarely, if ever, exercised, were heavy tobacco users and
frequent users of alcohol. They did talk about nutrition and tried to eat
a "variety of foods." To many of them, however, this meant nutrition,
not necessarily the content of the foods, such as sugar and salt, and use
of grease and fat.

At this point, blacks valued the medical system and used it as an option. Many said: "It is not like the old days when we could not see a doctor. He knows best sometimes." Their increasing use of biomedicine has expanded their knowledge and has become a part of their belief system. Additional information has added to their knowledge system and has entered into their explanatory models of health and illness behavior. Since the 1960s they have been able to experience medicine in a way that, before then, was impossible. Thus, they are culturally linking to the system through their changing beliefs, symbols, and knowledge associated with using this option for illness. Their linkages, however, remain differentiated from those of whites in Coberly.

As blacks have made these linkages to the medical systems, their cultural repertory related to health care has been restructured. This transformation of their beliefs and knowledge has taken place through the increasing dominance of the medical system in their lives. While they are active interpreters of medical information, their voice is rarely heard in the health planning and policy arena. They remain numbers with no authority in a hierarchial structure that continues to perpetuate inequality and injustice for the less powerful members of southern society. Since most of their knowledge is of health care providers, they are the key linkages among the health systems in contact, in praxis.

POWER, KNOWLEDGE, AND MEDICAL DOMINANCE

In 1822 James Madison warned: "A popular Government without popular information, or the means of acquiring it, is but a Prologue to a Farce or a Tragedy; or perhaps both. . . . a people who mean to be their own governors, must arm themselves with the power which knowledge gives."

Health systems are reproduced and transformed at the intersection between power and knowledge, between the cultures and structures of the hierarchial systems of a society. The nature and production of discourse and meaning in medicine "is at once controlled, selected, organized and redistributed according to certain procedures" that maintain power—power through knowledge (Foucault 1972:216). Historical struggle takes place in discourse, and in critiquing medical knowledge the power of the medical system is called into question.

Medicalization has become a dominant discourse as more social and cultural problems are placed within the Western medical model, thus increasing its power and, at the same time, decreasing the options people have to solve their "health" problems. Through expanding and contracting the knowledge base of people, it impacts the economic, political, and cultural aspects of the complex system. It increases the reliance of people upon urban-based medicine which, in Georgia, does not seem to be working particularly in the case of infant mortality, strokes, and hypertension. Medicalization is a historical process that impinges on population, such as poor blacks in the South, and through increasing linkages is bringing about transformation in their culture. Consequently, increased linkages, while changing behavior and beliefs, have not significantly changed the health status of blacks in the South. Epidemiological knowledge highlights the problems statistically. Medical personnel talk about "lifestyle" as the problem, and policymakers, while often agreeing with medical personnel, don't know what to do to solve "those people's problem."

The first section of this paper demonstrated that there is a problem in terms of the health and well-being of blacks, especially poor blacks in the South. Whose problem is it, who will solve it, and how will it be solved? By framing the problem within a complex systems approach using both micro- and macrolevel data and by examining the continuities and discontinuities of the culture and structure of the discourses found on different levels of the hierarchial society that we live in in the South, we can further ask, at what level can the problem be solved? Two frames come to mind. One frame concentrates on "lifestyle"— the behavior of "the other." This metaphor perpetuates the constitutive culture of policymakers and medical personnel. It may be more correctly described as a "problem setting" exercise rather than a "problem solving" one, making sense within the structure and culture of the most powerful, who therefore continue to collect data that uphold their constructed reality of the other. The solution within this frame is to change the behavior of poor blacks since, these policymakers reason, it is *their* behavior that is causing the problem. Without discussing who benefits from this solution, it should be pointed out that this type of thinking and acting, including setting priorities for the "public good" on the part of the powerful, constitutes the social and cultural construction of racism in southern society.

Another frame-setting problem starts at the societal level and questions the culture and structure that allows inequality and injustice to continue in the health system; it questions the us-them dichotomy. Such a solution for improving the health status of blacks in the south would create opportunities for increased reciprocal linkages that would trigger changes in the whole complex system. Making changes "beyond life-style" would activate and empower people, who have a right and an obligation in a democracy to change society to meet their health needs and to determine their own destiny. Empowering people and their communities to exercise their rights, I predict, would increase health status among blacks. Transformations that allow blacks on the local level to put more motion in the system will be more successful.

Alternative solutions that frame health problems within the multiplicities and complexities of the structural and cultural elements in a complex system are the "path" of transformations in health. One critical path that must be taken, however, is to hear the voice of the people on the bottom of the hierarchy, the microlevel, and not let the knowledge, voice, and authority of the dominant class determine the organization of the complex systems. Similar conclusions can be drawn for the authoritative discourses of social scientists who reflect their own culture and structure. Our constructed reality holds only fragments of truth. The Western medical model, with its own structure and culture, is one system of knowledge that solves a finite domain of health problems very well. There are other ways of organizing knowledge to solve health problems that may, if we look to the periphery, provide awareness based on the other's experiences, that can give us creative answers for solving health problems beyond the domain of biomedicine. Southern blacks cannot continue to be the object of medical practices but must also become the subject in a dialectical game toward equality and social justice within the health care system in the American South.

NOTES

1. I want to thank several people who helped me with the writing, editing, and typing of this paper. Terrie Lofton worked with me diligently to find the latest epidemiological information on blacks in the United States and in Georgia. She also provided invaluable comments on the content of the paper.

Similarly, Beatriz Morales read the manuscript with her usual critical mind and made invaluable comments and suggestions.

2. The black population referred to in this chapter is poor. While the number of middle-class blacks is increasing, the majority remains poor. I should mention that while more blacks dropped below the poverty line in the 1980s, a portion also began to earn higher incomes than ever before and joined the middle and upper-middle class. This process has led to what Landry (1987) has called "the two Black Americas." He refers to the underclass and the "buppies." This black schism reflects a growing income inequality among blacks. It is growing faster among blacks than among whites.

3. I have found that there are many similar behavioral characteristics between poor blacks and poor whites in the American South (see Hill 1988).

4. Helen is a pseudonym used to protect the confidentiality of the informant.

Killing the Medical Self-Help Tradition Among African Americans: The Case of Lay Midwifery in North Carolina, 1912–1983

Holly F. Mathews

In 1988 the citizens of North Carolina were shocked to learn that their annual infant mortality rate of 12.6 per thousand live births was the worst in the nation.[1] Even more disturbing was the fact that nonwhites averaged 18.7 deaths per thousand live births, a rate far worse than that found in all of the industrialized nations of the West and in many Third World countries (Bloch 1990:A-1; North Carolina 1988:2–1). The governor expressed outrage and pledged to renew the state's efforts to combat infant deaths. He offered no specific remedies, however, and additional funding allocations for maternal and child health programs were not immediately forthcoming. This left state health officials in a quandary. Why was infant mortality still a problem in 1988, and how could it be solved?

Facts were marshaled in the quest for explanation. Officials noted that the highest infant death rates occurred in the eastern third of the state in predominantly rural, poor counties with large nonwhite populations (North Carolina 1988). These counties also faced a severe shortage of available medical personnel. While the average physician-to-patient ratio in the state improved from 1 to 911 in 1978 to 1 to 637 in 1987, the ratio in the eastern counties declined, averaging in nonwhite areas one physician for every 3,550 people. One county of twenty-five thousand people had no resident physicians at all (*What If . . . ? School of Medicine Has Contributed* 1990; Center for Health Services Research and Development 1988).

In the absence of funds to create new programs, state officials began to suggest that local lay health advocates be recruited to assist county personnel in reaching out to rural women with information about pregnancy (Center for Health Services Research and Development 1989). It was strikingly ironic that the year in which this solution was proposed was the very year in which the lay midwifery tradition in rural North Carolina appeared finally to have been eradicated.

The first state Board of Health survey in 1917 documented the existence of nine thousand midwives in North Carolina (Wall 1956:362). In 1925 the state led the nation in the number of practicing midwives with sixty-five hundred. These midwives delivered one-third of all babies born that year, and of all midwife-assisted births, 20 percent were white and 80 percent were black (Hobbs 1927:27). Another survey by the Board of Health between 1929 and 1931 located 4,266 midwives who delivered 23,234 or 31 percent of the 74,743 babies born in 1931. While 88 percent of the white women delivering were attended by physicians, only 31 percent of black women had these services (North Carolina State Board of Health 1932:3). The percentage of births attended by midwives had declined to 24.6 in 1940, and still further to 10.9 by 1950, when the number of registered midwives had dropped to 915 (Lamb and Swindell 1954:7, 13). Twenty years later only fifty registered midwives survived, representing thirty-nine of the state's one hundred counties and accounting for 2,511 deliveries in 1970 (Warren 1972:1). By 1980, when the North Carolina General Assembly began to consider prohibiting the practice of lay midwifery, only 10 registered midwives continued to practice (Reid 1980:8B), and in 1988 there were no official records of any deliveries in North Carolina by lay midwives (North Carolina 1988).

After almost seventy years of systematic effort, state officials succeeded in eliminating the only officially sanctioned lay health practitioners in North Carolina—the midwives, most of whom were black women living in rural areas delivering black babies. A brief review of the history of the traditional practice of lay midwives in eastern North Carolina and of the state's orchestrated efforts to eliminate them from the health system will serve to illustrate how issues of race, class, and gender impacted upon maternal and child health policy in North Carolina in the years between 1912 and 1983.

Interviews conducted in eastern North Carolina with elderly, retired "granny" midwives, as black midwives were called throughout the South, reveal that much of their traditional practice involved the very activities that state health officials were seeking to promote in 1989 (see also Dougherty 1978a, 1978b; Mongeau et al. 1961; and Susie 1988 for additional descriptions). The traditional midwife was "engaged" by a woman patient in the early stages of her pregnancy. From that point on, the midwife visited her home regularly, instructing her in proper nutrition for herself and the expected baby and preparing her for the birth process. At the time of delivery, the midwife would assist the mother through labor; afterward, she or her assistant would usually stay on with the new mother for one to two weeks to help with housework, do the cooking, and care for the infant until the mother recovered completely. This postnatal care enabled the mother to devote her energies exclusively to the infant in the crucial time immediately following delivery. As one retired midwife from Halifax County, North Carolina, described her duties:

> You teach them how to take care of themselves, to keep the house clean and proper for a baby, 'bout good food to eat so they'll have good milk and how to make the baby's clothes. Then you get ready for the birthin' so they won't be scared and you be there with them any time of day or night. Lord, I've been called at some strange times. But when that baby's comin' there ain't nothin' for it but to do it. And stay—stayin' after, that's the thing. That's when they really need you more than in the catchin' 'cause after is when the tiredness sets in and they're weak and that's when the baby prone to sickness. So I'se always been one to stay as long as they needed me; to help clean, cook, and sometimes show 'em what to do with that little baby. And I never lost but one baby in all my days of work.

Most midwives learned their trade through long apprenticeships to older, established midwives, usually their kinswomen. The apprenticed girl would accompany her mentor on visits to pregnant women, sew and clean for them, and stay with them after their babies were born. After years of attending births and after having her own first child, the apprentice could begin to assist at deliveries and eventually answer night calls for the senior midwife. When the senior midwife decided to retire, she would officially hand over her practice and patients to her chosen successor. In this way, the traditions of midwifery were passed from generation to generation and continuity in belief and practice were maintained.

At the turn of the century, the birth process in rural southern communities was controlled largely by women. Although the majority of lay midwives registered by the state of North Carolina in 1917 were black

(Hardin 1925; Wall 1956), they attended births for white, Indian, and black rural mothers and were respected by all for their dedication and ability (North Carolina State Board of Health 1932:3; Myers 1921:7). The spiritual authority with which the midwife's role was invested added to the admiration and esteem she accrued over the course of her career. Because the passing on of the tradition to either a female relative or a young woman who had received a special calling from God was a matter of grave importance, the lines of authority and transmission of midwifery skills and lore were tightly controlled. Midwives earned their positions of respect as the keepers of life in rural communities.

Outside of the rural South and in larger metropolitan areas within the region, the tradition of midwifery began to decline rapidly after the 1920s as the professionalization of medicine as a whole and the development of the field of obstetrics in particular progressed (c.f., Devitt 1979a and 1979b; Kobrin 1966; Litoff 1978, 1986; Susie 1988). Medical associations began recognizing obstetrics and gynecology as legitimate specialties, and a host of new technological instruments to aid in birth were developed. In addition, the growth of hospitals after 1910 opened up new maternity wards that were more accessible to a broader segment of the population (Vogel 1980). As physicians began increasingly to enter the birth arena, midwives came to be seen as competitors both because they monopolized the pool of low-income women who were needed in classroom teaching (Kobrin 1966:357; Williams 1912) and because they depressed the status and economic rewards accorded to the new specialty (Kobrin 1966:358; Proctor 1923:116). As long as uneducated midwives controlled the delivery process, physicians feared that the specialty of obstetrics and gynecology would receive little standing in the medical profession. De Lee (1915:117), a leading physician, wrote:

> It is a general complaint of obstetric teachers that young physicians do not adopt obstetrics for their specialty. That the work is hard, that obstetrics is a jealous and exacting mistress, is appreciated, but neither deters the young man, because the science and art of obstetrics are the most interesting and gratifying in medicine. What does deter him, and it may be said without disparagement, is the fact that his arduous labor and sacrifice of time, of comfort and self, are not appreciated and required with respect and renumeration . . . as long as the medical profession tolerates this brand of infamy, the midwife, the public will not be brought to realize that there is a high art in obstetrics and that it must pay as well for it as for surgery.

Public interest in problems of maternal and child health intensified as part of the general social reform movement active in this country at the turn of the century. Advocates of such reform began to realize that improvements in care given at birth would be the key to the long-term health of the child and possibly of the family. As a result, they urged the adoption of licensing and training programs for midwives active both in city slums among large immigrant populations and in the rural South (Devitt 1979a:83). This push for licensure threatened physicians who, as Devitt writes, "feared that certification would lend permanence and legitimacy to this as yet tenuous trade" (1979a:83) and bring their own practices under increasing regulation, especially if they, like their counterparts in Europe, should be required by law to aid midwives in an emergency (Devitt 1979a:93).

Physicians and public health officials at the time differed in their opinions about solutions to what they termed the "midwife problem." Most specialists in obstetrics, particularly in the northeastern United States, wanted the midwife outlawed (Noyes 1912), although some, such as Ziegler (1913), favored their gradual abolition through stricter regulation. In the South, where most rural areas were badly underserviced, many public health officials and obstetricians recognized that midwives could not immediately be eliminated and so proposed that they be given training until such time as an adequate supply of physicians became available (Hardin 1925; Myers 1921).

By the 1920s the last two strongholds of midwifery were black women of the South and immigrant women of the North (Litoff 1978; Susie 1988). Physicians played upon ethnic and racial stereotypes to portray these midwives to the rest of the country as ignorant, backward, and superstitious and argued that they spread disease with their filthy customs and practices in attending birth and thus contributed to high levels of maternal and child mortality. Susie (1988:5) describes a popular ad circulated by physicians at the time noting that it "showed three midwives: an Italian woman, a Southern black woman, and an Irish woman, each dressed in dark, old-world garb and framed against an even darker background—a clear contrast to the slim, fashionable women of the adjoining ads." The caption read: "A typical Italian midwife practicing in one of our cities. They bring with them filthy customs and practices. A 'granny' of the far south. Ignorant and superstitious, a survival of the "magic doctors" of the West coast of Africa. . . . Surely, it might have been this woman of Irish-American parentage who is quoted as having said: 'I am too old to clean, too weak to wash, too blind to sew; but, thank God, I can still put my neighbors to bed.' " Similarly, an obstetrician from Alabama, writing in the state medical journal, described the black midwife as "the typical, old, gin-fingering, guzzling midwife with her pockets full of forcing drops, her mouth full of snuff, her fingers full of dirt and her brains full of arrogance and superstition" (Gewin 1906:629), while a colleague in Mississippi wrote a similar piece depicting these midwives as "filthy and ignorant and not far removed from the jungles of Africa" (Underwood 1926:683).

As medical professionals worked to define childbirth as a dangerous and potentially pathological event that could not be left to women—especially ignorant immigrant and black midwives—the hospital was promoted as the best place to give birth, and the professional, white male gynecologist was deemed the only appropriate specialist to attend at delivery (c.f., Litoff 1986:12). J. S. Brewer, a physician in Roseboro, North Carolina, wrote (1928:6): "Child bearing has for so long a time been looked upon as an entirely normal and physiologic affair that the idea that it borders closely on the pathologic and in an apparently increasing number of cases is actually pathologic seems hard to get across to the lay mind." Midwives were blamed directly for the failure of women and of the general public to adopt modern standards of medical care for delivery. As Brewer added (1928:6), women suffering the complications of labor would assume everything was normal if the "old black mammy midwife" said that it was.

According to Susie (1988:3), two inducements that lured women away from midwives were pain-saving drugs and time-saving forceps, inventions monopolized by physicians. And although women with the financial wherewithal responded to the appeal of medically attended deliveries in increasing numbers, physician-directed obstetrics did not result in the following years in safer maternity (Devitt 1979b:182; Litoff 1986:5). Nonetheless, as the professionalization of obstetrics advanced, professional medical societies began to seek the complete elimination of the lay midwife.

Yet for most lower-class women, especially immigrant women residing in urban slums and nonwhite women residing in the rural South, physician-assisted births were not a realistic option. Reformers of the era did succeed in securing some measure of assistance for these women with the passage by Congress in 1921 of the Sheppard-Towner Maternity and Infancy Act, which subsidized midwife education programs, mainly in the southern states (Devitt 1979a:86). By 1927 there were 10,881 midwives enrolled in classes in fourteen states, and these programs spread to another fifteen states by 1929 (Devitt 1979a:87). The White House Conference on Child Health and Protection held in 1932 found that in the South "the Negro midwives have shown themselves eager and willing to avail themselves of such educational advantages as have been offered to them . . . by state boards of health" and concluded on the basis of an examination of available statistics that midwives in general showed "very favorable maternal mortality rates . . . and remarkably low rates for the mothers attended by trained and supervised midwives." This record was even more impressive since midwives uniformly attended poorer women who were more likely to live in crowded and unsanitary residences and have poorer health than the women attended by physicians (Devitt 1979b:170). In addition, midwives in areas as diverse as New York City and rural Mississippi proved themselves effective as lay health advocates. They assisted in bringing thousands of women into clinics for prenatal care, censusing the population for venereal disease, promoting better sanitation practices, and in rounding up children for immunization (Devitt 1979b:179).

Many physicians, however, viewed passage of the Sheppard-Towner Act, which was officially opposed by the American Medical Association, as tantamount to the institution of socialism and the beginnings of widespread government control over the medical profession. Due to their vociferous opposition, the act lapsed in 1929 (Devitt 1979a:93). Nonetheless, training courses for midwives continued, and many obstetricians, fearful that lay midwifery would become institutionalized, began to articulate a path of compromise by voicing support for the use of the nurse-midwives—registered nurses with advanced training in midwifery—as licensed birth attendants. Taussig argued in the *Wisconsin Medical Journal* in 1917 that nurses could, through their professional organizations and established positions in the medical hierarchy, be self-regulated. Consequently, there would be no further need for government intervention in the medical care associated with birth, and physicians, charged with training and supervising nurse-midwives, could depend upon their allegiance. This emerging alliance between physicians and nurse-midwives marked the beginning of a division of interests between the cadre of white, professional nurses and the upper-middle-class women who would use their services and poorer women who would continue to rely on the largely immigrant and nonwhite force of lay midwives for assistance with birth. This latter group was, in a sense, doomed to lose the struggle for legitimacy since, as Devitt (1979b:182) writes, "The immigrant origins of most midwives outside the South and the similarly disadvantaged status of the Black midwives kept them from establishing the schools and institutions necessary to resist the physicians' attack."

Several independent events in the 1920s would act together to lead to the rapid decline of the lay midwife. These included the application of increasingly stringent regulations to midwives by local health boards, the passage by Congress of restrictive immigration acts that limited the number of new midwives arriving in the country, and changing attitudes on the part of the upper-middle classes favoring smaller family size and increasing medical intervention in birth as a sign of progressive social attitudes. Yet the advancement of the nurse-midwife as substitute for the lay midwife would never happen to the extent predicted in this decade. And the division of interests that split women along the lines of class and race would surface again in the final debates about the elimination of lay midwifery conducted in southern legislatures in the 1970s and 1980s.

The process leading to the elimination of the lay midwife in North Carolina was a long one influenced in many ways by national debates and yet shaped as well by the particular characteristics of the state and its population. Although midwife training began in North Carolina as early as 1772 and continued to grow rapidly through the first part of the twentieth century, physicians were adamant about the need to eliminate the practice. War was declared on the granny midwife by the General Assembly of the state in 1912 with passage of a law granting any county board of health the power to license and control midwives (Wall 1956:362). Five years passed before Rocky Mount, a small town in eastern North Carolina, became the first community in the South to pass and enforce a law making it illegal for any midwife in the city to practice her profession without having passed a satisfactory examination in the elementary principles of midwifery. The town was also one of the first to conduct free courses of instruction for midwives and charged them no fees for the examination or permits issued (North Carolina State Board of Health 1917:108). In that same year, the state passed a law requiring all county health boards to register midwives. This was thought to be the first step toward their eventual elimination (Wall 1956:362). In an article in the *Southern Medical Journal* in 1925, a North Carolina physician named E. R. Hardin (1925:348) argued that their elimination was crucial because these midwives were, except in rare cases, "ignorant, untrained, incompetent women, and some of the results of their incompetence are unnecessary deaths and blindness of infants, avoidable invalidism, suffering and death of mothers." What was needed, he argued, was the better training of physicians in obstetrics and the elimination of midwives like those in his home county of Robeson, North Carolina, who were "far below the European midwife in intelligence and no training under the sun could make her a competent obstetric attendant" (1925:350).

However, physicians and public health officials in North Carolina realized that the immediate elimination of black midwives was not feasible since large rural black populations were not allowed entry to white hospitals, little medical training was available to provide black physicians and nurses, and relatively few health alternatives were open to the population. As Katherine Myers (1921:7) wrote of midwifery in eastern North Carolina in 1921: "The distressing lack of medical service in our ten super-rural counties, the concentration of physicians in towns, bad roads, absence of telephone connections, poverty, ignorance, and custom—all have combined to foster a service enormously powerful for good or evil." State health officials also realized that the underserviced rural population would not willingly give up the midwife without some alternative service available (see also Susie 1988). Consequently, North Carolina turned to regulation and training as an intermediate step.

After passage of the 1917 law, many counties began to hold local registration and training sessions for midwives. The majority of the nine thousand midwives registered by 1924 were over age 40, 15 percent were over age 70, and the median age of registered midwives was 66 (Myers 1921; Mongeau et al. 1961). The highest ratio of midwife-attended births occurred in the eastern coastal plain counties, where the majority of midwives registered were black, and in the western mountain ones, where the majority of midwives were white (Hardin 1924; Hobbs 1927:27). Because of the substantially greater populations and higher birth rates in the eastern counties, registered black midwives outnumbered by three to one those who were white. This figure corresponded to the percentages of women of the different races attended by midwives in 1925—70.55 percent of blacks and 14.09 percent of whites (Hobbs 1927:27). It is not surprising then that the twenty-three North Carolina counties with the worst maternal and infant death records were all in the eastern part of the state (North Carolina State Board of Health 1927:29).

By 1921, as Myers (1921:8) wrote, state law required four things of midwives: "registration, use of silver nitrate solution, reporting of cases of opthalmia neonatorum, reporting of births." In addition, twenty-five county health departments had instituted courses of instruction for midwives based on a syllabus prepared and outlined by the Bureau of Public Health Nursing and Infant Hygiene (Myers 1921:8). In another fifty-two counties throughout the state, public health nurses held seventy-three training conferences, which were attended by 898 midwives, of whom 106 were white and 792 were black. The conferences involved the registration of midwives, an explanation of state laws regarding midwifery regulation, and instruction in proper delivery techniques and the importance of prenatal care (Vaughan 1919:13–14). The nurses also discussed the mental attitude and qualifications, character, physical fitness, and habits desirable in midwives because, as Myers (1921:8) reported: "Their status and relation to physicians need defining especially in the 'black belt,' and every effort is made to inculcate in them a feeling of regard and respect for his opinion and advice, and to look upon him as their friend and counselor." Nurses also taught the midwives how to prepare a bag of supplies and carry out proper sanitation procedures before birth, and instructed them about the complications of pregnancy that required the notification of a physician.

In 1924 the counties voluntarily adopted more rigid control over midwives by passing laws that required permits to practice, which were given only after proper training and examination (Rankin 1925:13–14). These permits had to be renewed annually, which required recertification, and they were subject to revocation if midwives were reported to have violated any of a series of rules specifying the proper limits of their activities (North Carolina State Board of Health 1925). In addition, county boards of health often passed strict regulations governing the behavior of midwives. In Durham County, North Carolina, for example, the midwife was told that she had to refuse a case when the patient had experienced severe labors with earlier confinements; when she had had fits or convulsions; when she was a dwarf or deformed, had syphilis, or was vomiting badly; when there was bleeding before labor or swelling in the hands or feet; or when the patient had dizzy spells (Lougee 1964). In addition, the county specified that the midwife had to be a woman of good character and in good health, clean in body and clothes and about home and patient, and ready and willing to obey the law and improve her work. To be certified with a permit, the midwife must have tested negative for venereal disease, have attended maternity clinics and meetings at the health department, and have complete equipment as required (Lougee 1964). In most counties, the public health nurse approved pregnant women for attendance by a midwife. Midwives were then supervised directly by county nurses or local physicians. In this way, the midwife's activities in attending the woman and the outcome of the birth could be monitored. Midwives judged to be negligent in their duty by taking on cases without permission, by failing to call in a physician for complications, or by violating the proper standards of sanitation and care could be dismissed from practice and have their licenses revoked.

The state board of health declared 70 to be the mandatory retirement age for lay midwives. County health departments were encouraged to recruit new midwives who were younger, literate, and thus more likely to be amenable to training and supervision and to discontinue gradually the licensing of older, illiterate midwives who were more likely to operate independently of supervision. The passage of the Shepherd-Townson Act provided the state with funds to establish health districts under the supervision of nurses and to pay an additional twenty individual county nurses to assist in the registration, training, and monitoring of lay midwives (Cooper 1937:6). After Congress passed the Social Security Act in 1936, additional funds were made available through the U.S. Children's Bureau for the development of a state plan for maternal and infant health. At that time, 68 percent of black women in the state were still attended in birth by midwives, and the infant death rate continued to be high. By the end of 1936, the state had established 117 prenatal medical centers staffed by local physicians and one or more public health nurse and, when available, by pediatricians, obstetricians, and dentists in forty of the one hundred counties (North Carolina State Board of Health 1936:14). In addition, eight nurses were paid exclusively by the state Board of Health to hold midwife classes in forty-five counties.

These nurses personally examined and instructed about fifteen hundred midwives (Cooper 1937:8).

In describing the progress made by programs of licensing and training in Robeson County in the 1920s, E. R. Hardin (1925:350), the vocal critic of midwives, wrote that "the majority have made a creditable showing when quizzed and have demonstrated the manner in which they use the silver nitrate solution which is furnished by the state for the babies' eyes. . . . the midwives have all been given a list of the things they should take with them on their cases. Most of them have willingly supplied themselves with the necessary equipment, and at a recent meeting when they were asked to bring their bags for inspection, the majority of them made a good showing." While most state health officials viewed regulation and supervision as a step toward eliminating midwives, many of the midwives themselves were grateful for the interest of physicians in their practice and for the opportunities to learn more about birth and gain access to new equipment and materials. Reports from various counties in North Carolina from the 1920s through the 1950s indicate that midwives attended meetings and training sessions regularly, complied for the most part with regulations regarding attendance at home births, and compiled records for infant mortality no worse and sometimes better than those of physicians attending home deliveries in the state (United States 1932).

Lay midwives enjoyed a record of success, and rural areas continued to need their services. Yet rapid changes were beginning to endanger the survival of this trained cadre of lay midwives, as Mongeau et al. (1961) documented in their study of black midwifery in rural North Carolina in the late 1950s. Hospital facilities and young obstetric and gynecological specialists were becoming increasingly available to whites in metropolitan areas. In rural areas the older family physicians were retiring or dying and not being replaced. Opportunities for traditional midwives to work with physicians and learn new techniques were disappearing at the very time when whites in urban and rural areas were beginning to embrace the values and attitudes of modern medicine about the virtues of hospital births.

Local county health department regulations were slowly altering the traditional makeup of the midwife pool as mandatory retirements continued, requirements for relicensing were stiffened, and permits for new practitioners were rejected in increasing numbers. Midwife training in the early 1950s, for example, changed from locally led classes to centralized instruction in regional institutes. Attendance was restricted to midwives under the age of 60 who were able to read and write, pay for their own room and board, remain for the full two weeks, and who were willing to undergo complete physical examinations with chest X rays. A total of 277 midwives, for example, attended the two institutes held in 1953. This represented 32 percent of those known to be practicing at the time. The final report on the institutes predicted that the number of active midwives would continue to decline as more of them reached retirement age. Consequently, efforts at local-level training and supervision were deemed to be no longer cost effective or necessary (Lamb and Swindell 1954:9).

During the latter part of the 1950s, the state began to question seriously the need for lay midwives, arguing that the goal of extending hospital services to every county would make medically assisted care for all mothers a reality in the near future (Lamb and Swindell 1954:14). In 1964 the last permit for midwifery was issued by the North Carolina Department of Human Resources, and by 1970 only fifty registered midwives remained in the state, mostly in the rural eastern counties (Wayne 1971).

In 1977, however, a renewed interest in midwifery on the part of young, middle- and upper-class white women resulted in the submission of new applications for licenses in many counties in the more urbanized areas of the state. During that same year, the North Carolina General Assembly passed the Sunset Law (North Carolina 1977, chap. 712, sec. 334), which provided for the automatic review of licensing laws by repealing approximately one-third of them each biennium. In addition, the law called for a newly created Governmental Evaluation Commission to conduct a performance evaluation of each licensing program, hold public hearings on the matter, and make a recommendation to the General Assembly about whether to terminate, reconstitute, or continue it (Solberg 1979:5). The date for the repeal of the midwifery licensing law was set for 1 July 1981. In the meantime, a moratorium was declared prohibiting the licensing of any new midwives until a ruling on repeal could be obtained (Reid 1980; Solberg 1979:5).

The debate generated strong sentiments on all sides of the issue and, as Queen (1982:14) wrote, "caused a showdown of state health officials, physicians, nurse practitioners, health consumers, and would-be lay midwives over the need for trained attendants for childbirth outside a hospital." Proponents of repeal argued that the granny midwives were poor, illiterate, superstitious, and responsible for inhibiting rural North Carolinians from seeking proper medical care. In 1971 Dr. Theodore Scurletis, director of the personal health division of the state Board of Health articulated the position later voiced in the public hearings: "The granny midwife has no place in the care of people today. She was ignorant and often dangerous. What was a logical solution for health care in the 1930s is impractical today. Then you had a lack of hospitals, doctors, and sophisticated methods of delivery. But today that isn't true" (Wayne 1971). The *North Carolina Health Bulletin* reaffirmed these sentiments in a 1972 review article on midwifery when the editor concluded: "The demise of the practice of the granny-type midwife signals a victory for modern health care in the state. After centuries of her practice and generations of battling her existence, the granny is gone—hopefully, never to return" (Warren 1972:1).

Nonetheless, opponents of midwifery recognized that serious health problems still plagued rural areas in the state and acknowledged that physician shortages were not likely to fill the gap in the immediate future since North Carolina had one of the nation's lowest physician-to-population ratios (North Carolina 1971). As a solution, many health officials advocated a return to an idea first proposed by physicians in 1920—that lay midwives be eliminated in favor of certified nurse-midwives (Warren 1972). The extensive use of nurse-midwives, it was argued, could help to lower the high national and even higher North Carolina infant mortality rate (Warren 1972:3; Warren 1974:2).

Yet, as critics pointed out, there were no existing nurse-midwifery training and certification programs operating in the state. Moreover, nurse-midwifery as defined by law required the nurse to practice under the supervision of a physician and to attend only deliveries done in hospitals (Warren 1972:2). Consequently, so long as physicians and hospitals remained unavailable to rural women, the added presence of the nurse-midwife would do little to help them unless the state agreed to license nurse-midwives to conduct home deliveries.

In 1980, the North Carolina Governmental Evaluation Commission recommended that the practice of lay midwifery be outlawed but that certified nurse-midwives be allowed to attend women who wanted home deliveries (Reid 1980). This recommendation, which was to go to the

General Assembly, was aired at a public hearing in March of that year (Reid 1980). The North Carolina Medical Society opposed all home births, refused to support the measure, and began an intense lobbying campaign against it with legislators (Webb 1981). This campaign resulted in the introduction in the 1981 General Assembly of House Bill 695, "An Act to Abolish Lay Midwifery," which called for the complete elimination of midwifery in any form and therefore of home births as well (North Carolina 1981a:351). The bill was referred to committee.

In an effort to retain the availability of home birth, an all-woman House subcommittee met in 1981 to propose a substitute bill to the House Health Committee (Webb 1981). The substitute bill called for a two-year moratorium on the issuing of midwifery permits while the state Human Resources Department studied the state's policies on midwives in order to decide if they should be permitted to work outside of the hospital or not. The subcommittee chair, Representative Wilma Woodward of Raleigh, proposed that existing law be revised during the time the study was being conducted in order to allow nurse-midwives to deliver babies at home. The impetus behind her subcommittee's move was, she said, the feeling that "it was crucial for women to have assistance if they *choose* birthing at home" (Webb 1981:14; emphasis mine).

This statement is illuminating because it reflects a fundamental shift in the framing of the midwifery question that occurred during the licensing debate. The central issue was reconceptualized by the House subcommittee to be one of choice and not access. As a result, the prior goal of the licensing program—the provision of access to prenatal and pregnancy care for underserved poor and rural women—was supplanted by a new one, the preservation of the right to home birth as an option of choice for women who already had medical care available to them. The five women on the House subcommittee were all white professionals from urban districts. Their genuine desire to protect women's interests by preserving the right to home birth in the face of strong challenges to it from the medical community cannot be doubted. Yet in forging a compromise that restricted such a right to women with access to registered nurse-midwives, this subcommittee sacrificed the interests of the numerically much larger group of poor, rural, and predominantly nonwhite women who were left without access to care. Thus the alliance with nurse-midwives, first proposed by physicians in the 1920s as a solution to the lay midwife problem, emerged victorious in the

1981 licensing debates in North Carolina. This happened in part because lay midwives had no base of support from which to lobby during this campaign. The surviving elderly, black midwives located mainly in rural eastern counties were not involved at all in the political process, while the young, urban white women desiring to practice lay midwifery were perceived by many lawmakers to comprise a small fringe group of "hippies" without credibility.

Eventually, a modified version of House Bill 695, renamed "An Act to Study and Regulate the Practice of Midwifery in North Carolina," was passed by the 1981 General Assembly (North Carolina 1981b, chap. 676, pg. 974). This compromise solution directed the secretary of the Department of Human Resources to study the issue of home delivery and report her findings to the 1983 General Assembly. In the interim, only nurse-midwives with permits from the Department of Human Resources and lay midwives who had held valid permits in North Carolina for ten years could attend home births. To receive permits, nurse-midwives had to be certified by the American College of Nurse-Midwives, demonstrate sufficient training and experience, and work under the supervision of a physician licensed to practice medicine (Queen 1982:14).

During the 1983 session of the General Assembly, permanent legislation on the midwife question was introduced in the form of House Bill 814, "An Act to Regulate the Practice of Midwifery" (North Carolina 1983b:351). Though the bill was opposed both by proponents of unregulated childbirth and the State Medical Society, the state did move to allow home births attended by nurse-midwives (Dellinger 1983:3). The House passed the bill on 13 July 1983, with a vote of sixty-nine in favor, including all of the nineteen women and seven black male representatives, and twenty-five against, with six absent (North Carolina 1983b:991). The bill passed in the Senate on 20 July 1983, with thirty-six voting in favor, including all four women and the one black man in the Senate, and two against (North Carolina 1982:854).

This bill specified the definitions and requirements for midwifery in North Carolina (Article 10A to North Carolina 1977, Chaps. 90–97). Midwives could give care outside a hospital but only under the supervision of a physician practicing obstetrics. Approval to practice nurse-midwifery had to come from a joint subcommittee of the Board of Medical Examiners and the Board of Nursing, which was to include two midwives and two obstetricians who had worked with them. To be eligible to practice, applicants had to be certified by the American College of Nurse-Midwives. Although the act did not specify that midwives had to be registered nurses, the American College of Nurse-Midwives did require this degree to issue its certification. However, the door was left open for future certification of those other than registered nurses (Delinger 1983:3).

Unapproved practice of midwifery was named a misdemeanor, and a grace period was declared from the law's effective date of 1 October 1983 until 1 April 1984, for midwives authorized under the repealed law to leave the field of practice. Of the ten licensed lay midwives allowed to continue practicing under the 1981 interim law, none remained active in 1989. Yet the elimination of lay midwifery and the substitution of the practice of certified nurse-midwifery did not solve North Carolina's infant and maternal health problems as was predicted, nor has medical care replaced the services of the lay midwife in the rural and predominantly black areas of eastern North Carolina.

On the contrary, only twenty-six certified nurse-midwives were practicing in North Carolina in 1989 (Evans 1990:C-1); all were white women and the majority worked in urban areas. This shortage was due in part to the lack of a certified nurse-midwife training program in North Carolina, but also resulted, to a large extent, from the reluctance of obstetricians to undertake the supervision of these practitioners. Those midwives who did find placements, moreover, were usually limited to attending hospital births rather than home births because many obstetricians feared the possibility of lawsuits and were reluctant to pay the increased costs for liability coverage (nurse-midwives paid between $3,800 and $4,800 per year for such insurance in 1989). Today, seven years after the repeal of the lay midwifery licensing act, no primary care obstetrical service of any kind is available to many rural residents of the eastern coastal plain and the western mountain counties of the state. An article in the 8 November 1989 issue of the Washington, North Carolina, *Daily News* spotlighted this problem, pointing out that six counties in northeastern North Carolina were an obstetrics wasteland where only four doctors specializing in obstetrics and gynecology handled the births of about fifteen hundred babies each year. The article also concluded that the midwives had ceased to be a solution to the problem and called them "past history."

Those obstetricians remaining in rural practice, moreover, are being driven out rapidly by the rising costs of insurance. As a result, every year increasing numbers of rural, poor women are delivering in regional hospitals far distant from their homes. Without access to regular pre-natal care, it is not surprising that a high number of these deliveries have attendant complications like prematurity and low birth weight. Recent statistics indicate that the previously steady decline in infant mortality rates among nonwhites in the state is reversing as the proportion of pre-mature births and births to women who have never received prenatal care is increasing (North Carolina 1989).

And so the issue of maternal and infant health has come full circle in North Carolina. Now health officials must struggle to find solutions for a problem they thought they had solved at many points during the past seventy years. In late 1989 the North Carolina General Assem-bly decided to appropriate $10.5 million to combat infant mortality. It directed that a portion of this allocation should go to fund four teams of nurse-midwives to work in critically underserved counties in east-ern and western North Carolina (Evans 1990:C-1). The legislation also called for an assessment of the availability of prenatal care and support services for pregnant women in each county and a report on the fea-sibility of establishing a nurse-midwifery training program in the state (Evans 1990:C-1). While these efforts are a promising start, they are by no means a solution to the problems that affect thousands of women in these underserved counties.[2]

A more practical and immediate approach is being piloted in two rural counties by members of the Center for Health Services Research and Development at East Carolina University; it involves the recruitment and training of lay health advocates. The goal is to identify and instruct concerned community members, primarily those sought out by their neighbors for advice and help, in a comprehensive health and human services program that provides information and training in how to help others seek professional advice in order to meet health needs. One of the problems in implementing such a program, however, is the identification of community members who are respected advice givers. For outsiders to accomplish this, extensive ethnographic fieldwork is required. Even then, finding truly respected and knowledgeable volunteers is difficult.

Ironically, such a pool of registered and trained advocates for mater-nal and child health was available in all of the rural counties until well into the 1950s. Established in local communities, lay midwives were respected and admired for the services they rendered. Mechanisms for succession to the role and an apprenticeship system were operative, and relationships had been established between midwives, local physicians, and county health personnel. Clearly, this corps of lay workers would have proved an invaluable resource in these counties today. They could have been trained quickly and inexpensively to disseminate information on pregnancy and health care, to act as advocates for prenatal care, to notify physicians of problem pregnancies, to assist with deliveries and involve medical personnel in the process, and to aid health officials in recording and following up on births in rural areas. Yet decades of prejudice and discrimination directed toward these relatively poor, uneducated, and predominantly black midwives resulted in the forced elimination of this trained pool of lay health attendants who were, by the accounts of most physicians directly supervising them, extremely caring, competent, and responsible. Replacing them will be difficult because the tradition has been broken. And, as a result, an almost insurmountable gap now exists between medical personnel and rural residents in eastern North Carolina—a gap that affects the delivery of services for all health needs, not just those associated with pregnancy and infant care. Creative solutions are needed to solve these problems, and perhaps one of the most creative would be to return to the past and reexamine the ways in which traditional healers operated in rural communities so that better models for the recruitment and training of new lay health advocates can be developed.

NOTES

1. I thank Hans Baer and Ronald Hoag for helpful comments on an earlier version of this paper and Christy Garrison for assisting me with the collection of archive data. This paper is based on both historical and field research data collected in North Carolina between 1978 and 1990. I thank my informants, whose names have been changed to protect their confidentiality, for their gracious willingness to share their knowledge of birth with me.

2. After this article was written, the East Carolina University School of Nursing received permission from the University of North Carolina Board of Governors to establish the first registered nurse-midwife training program in the state. The program's mission will be to train nurse-midwives for underserved rural areas in North Carolina.

Community AIDS Education: Trials and Tribulations in Raising Consciousness for Prevention

Ira E. Harrison

How does a black community organize itself to deal with the AIDS epidemic?[1] Attempting to address this issue, I focus on African Americans living in various sections of a southeastern middle-sized metropolitan area called the Happy Valley.[2] Happy Valley is a southern upland working-class community (Gastil 1975:174–92). The black community has always been small. Unlike the large black populations in Southerntown (Dollard 1937), Plantation County (Rubin 1951), or Talladega (Kimball and Pearsall 1954), native blacks are relatively few, while other blacks migrate in and out of the Valley. Who does what in the black community, and what are the consequences for the Acquired Immunodeficiency Syndrome (AIDS) epidemic?

INTRODUCTION

AIDS adversely affects minorities, especially blacks. Nationally 78 percent of AIDS cases in children under 13 years old are minority cases: 54 percent black, 24 percent Hispanics. Hispanics and blacks comprise only 19 percent of the population. It is estimated that 71 percent of women with AIDS are minorities: 52 percent black, 19 percent Hispanic (Hopkins 1987). In Tennessee, whites comprise 83 percent of the population, blacks 15 percent, and Hispanics and others the remaining 2 percent. From 1982 to 1985, blacks comprised 18 percent of Tennessee's case load. In 1989 blacks comprised 26 percent of the state's case load. Seventy-five percent of children diagnosed with AIDS in 1989 were black. AIDS strikes black Tennesseans earlier than white Tennesseans: 39 percent of blacks are diagnosed before age 30, compared to 26 percent for whites. Black women of childbearing age are four times more likely to be HIV infected than white women (Ellis 1990). The events discussed in this paper predate these glaring statistics. They describe efforts to raise community consciousness about AIDS in one region in Tennessee.

EFFORTS TO IMPLEMENT AIDS PREVENTION EDUCATION AMONG AFRICAN AMERICANS IN HAPPY VALLEY

Any attempt to understand the AIDS prevention education effort or any other community event must be viewed in terms of historic and contemporary community processes. That is, recurring structural patterns of race, class, and gender must be recognized in order to understand the success or failure of community events like AIDS prevention education. I shall describe four AIDS prevention education events and examine these events in terms of historic regional patterns of race, class, and gender.

Historically, the black church has been a place of worship, a sanctuary, a spawning ground for political action, and a sponsor of health, housing, and welfare services (Nelson, Yorkley, Nelson 1971). It was my hunch that black ministers and the black church would provide the leadership and the direction in educating the black community about AIDS. Ministers are leaders in black communities, and thus I assumed that if AIDS were a threat to the community, they would lead the struggle against AIDS. Instead, I found that ministers did not lead, largely because they denied that AIDS posed a threat to the community.

The First Event

When I saw an article in the 3 January 1988 issue of the Happy Valley morning newspaper announcing that the local chapter of the American Red Cross would be presenting an AIDS education workshop for the Happy Valley Interdenomination Ministerial Alliance, I thought that my hunch was substantiated. Black ministers were going to assume leadership in the AIDS epidemic. The workshop was to be held at the Mighty Methodist Church, pastored by the Reverend Able. With the Reverend

Able's permission, I attended the monthly meeting of the Ministerial Alliance.

Twenty-seven black ministers heard a white male university professor say that AIDS is a disease that challenges the church to show care and concern and that the ministry should allow a person with AIDS to worship. Martha, a white female Red Cross nurse discussed the transmission of AIDS, showed an AIDS video tape ("Beyond Fear"), and revealed what the Red Cross was doing in AIDS education. Mary, a black county health social worker, discussed the high risk of blacks getting AIDS. She reported that as of 31 December 1987, five of forty-two reported AIDS cases from Happy Valley area were black males. This was 11 percent of the reported cases in a central city, where blacks constitute 14.6 percent of the population. She stated that Happy Valley was below the national average for AIDS incidence among blacks. However, AIDS cases were expected to rise because many blacks still thought that AIDS was a white gay disease. They did not use clean needles or practice safe sex. She reported that confidential blood testing for the AIDS virus was available at the Happy Valley County Health Department. The ministers were amused and puzzled by the virulence of the AIDS virus within the body and the wimpishness of the AIDS virus outside the body. The Red Cross had ample materials and resources and saw this workshop as an opportunity to affect the black community. Black ministers could help the Red Cross get the word to their people. The workshop ended with a feeling among health professionals that this was the beginning of AIDS prevention in the black community and that blacks needed to know more about AIDS. This was the beginning of my involvement in community AIDS activity.

I trained as a Red Cross AIDS educator and spoke on AIDS prevention at area schools and a Job Corps training program. Pearl, a black state university wellness director, and I videotaped and interviewed David, a dying black AIDS patient, on 9 March 1988. Fannie, his sister, wanted him to tell his story to help to prevent other blacks from getting AIDS.

The Second Event

Fannie, Chair of the Mighty Baptist Church's missionary committee, organized a seminar on "Acquired Immunodeficiency Syndrome" at her church on 13 May 1988. Fannie persuaded her daughter to ask her boss,

Dr. White, a white medical doctor, to speak on AIDS. After the Reverend Goodman, pastor of the Mighty Baptist Church, welcomed the forty-two men, women, and children, Pearl introduced Dr. White, who spoke on medical research on AIDS. Fannie and members of her family arranged a display on AIDS, and the videotape "AIDS and the Black Community" was shown. Martha, from the Red Cross, was present with her Red Cross display on AIDS. Most of the people present were Fannie's friends and people from her church.

Members of HELP were also present. HELP is a private nonprofit organization providing support groups for persons with AIDS, for families of those with AIDS, and for those HIV positive, as well as training, education, and counseling on matters dealing with AIDS. There were no blacks in HELP. I joined HELP to see what role HELP played in the AIDS efforts among blacks. HELP provided support for David. However, it has difficulty attracting blacks to serve in its programs. HELP is a new organization with no links to the black community. The two HELP executive committee members announced their services and welcomed people there to join them.

Martha, Pearl, Fannie, and I felt that we were on our way toward educating the black community. This program was basically Fannie's project, as she had been trying to get her minister to do something for the congregation on AIDS.

On 13 June 1988, one month after the seminar, David died of Kaposi's sarcoma at 38 years of age. As of 1 September 1988, three of seventeen deaths due to AIDS were black males! Eighteen percent of AIDS deaths in a metropolitan area, where blacks comprise only 14.6 percent of the central city and 1.6 percent of the surrounding county populations, were black males.

Martha was still concerned that AIDS education was not getting to blacks.[3] The Reverend Able, who also works as a health professional, reported that ministers are not dealing with it. A young man died of AIDS in his district; however, the family states he died of Crohn's disease.[4] This denial in the community was creating a block to the free flow of support and information. Homosexual and bisexual contact was the main transmission factor for AIDS in the Happy Valley area. There was a concern that the virus was getting into the heterosexual community. It was noted that denial impeded the activation of the customary mutual support among blacks for individuals and families when disease starts.

These observations were noted by the Reverend Able, Martha, and me in a 2 November 1988 meeting at the Red Cross building. We mapped a strategy to try to break through this denial and to tap a sensitivity to AIDS and to those in need. A spaghetti dinner for the congregations of the Mighty Baptist and the Mighty Methodist was planned, with invitations extended to the congregations of the black Ministerial Alliance. Thus a Baptist and a Methodist would jointly host the program.

The Third Event

Since we were anxious to get this program over before Christmas, we decided to host it on 1 December 1988, which was World AIDS Day. We were too late to get on early-morning local television shows, but messages were sent to area churches, and articles appeared in the Happy Valley newspapers.

The welcome and the purpose for the program were given by the Reverend Goodman and the Reverend Able, respectively, as the meeting was held in the Reverend Goodman's church. A black male representing the mayor's office endorsed our recognition of World AIDS Day. Dr. Rhoads, a physician with a master of public health degree (MD/MPH), the white county health officer, discussed the health challenge that AIDS poses. She also announced that Mary, the black social worker, would become a full-time AIDS education counselor when she returned from a special AIDS training program in Nashville within two weeks. This underscored the state's awareness of the growing AIDS epidemic in Tennessee and in this region. Martha described the AIDS challenge facing the communities. Fannie discussed the crisis that AIDS posed for families, while Dr. Sims, a black MD/MPH physician employed by an area energy company, outlined the AIDS challenge facing the medical profession. She was dynamic, and has gained areawide popularity as a good speaker on AIDS.

Only seventeen persons attended. Only three were neither program participants nor health professionals. It was clear that area ministers were not going to assume leadership in AIDS prevention education.

In 1989 burnout became evident. Dr. Sims, the popular public health physician, took a private-industry job in the Midwest. When I persuaded her to appear on our World AIDS Day Program, she asked: "What good is it going to do? I'm tired. No one's going to come! They have finally come up with a way to do away with us—drugs and AIDS and sex—and we are going to do it to ourselves. We are going to die out." Her attitude seemed similar to that exhibited by southern white physicians during the syphilis epidemic in the 1930s (Jones 1981). Pearl began devoting less time to AIDS and became more involved in activities related to other sexual transmitted diseases, alcohol, and drugs.

Meanwhile, I became chair of the NAACP's Citizen's Development Committee, and suggested that AIDS prevention education be our priority. The two other members of the committee, who are both black (Betty, a businesswoman, and Joan, a nurse), concurred. It took us two months to plan our meeting.

The Fourth Event

The program was called a public forum, "AIDS in Black Happy Valley: A Family Affair: Help and Hope," sponsored by the Happy Valley NAACP and supported by the Media Center of Hill Baptist Church, the Happy Valley County Department of Health, the Tennessee Department of Health and Environment, the Red Cross, and HELP. Joan notified the two newspapers, the major television stations, and the three radio stations that blacks listen to frequently. Betty secured the church auditorium and sent letters from the president of the NAACP and fliers to fifty-five churches and area black social, fraternal, and sororal organizations. I delivered fliers to Happy Valley College, the University Black Cultural Center, my barbershop, my cleaners, the NAACP meeting, and my church. I helped to prepare Fannie and her family for their presentations and spoke with reporters of both newspapers. The evening newspaper wrote an excellent front-page article, with pictures of Fannie and her family, announcing the public forum.

Willie, the state minority AIDS coordinator from Nashville, made a special trip to Happy Valley for this community event, held on 12 October 1989. Fannie and each member of her family told how they had to deal with AIDS as David—their brother, uncle, and cousin—died from AIDS. Her brother's lover was present and became disruptive, loud, and angry. Fannie defused a potentially nasty situation by publicly reaching out to him as she has done continuously. He finally quieted down. Mary reported that confidential blood testing and AIDS counseling was available at the County Health Department. Martha reviewed Red Cross activities in AIDS prevention and training. Both Mary and Martha had assembled AIDS education displays. Willie related the state's readiness to support County Health Department testing, counseling, and activities. The state also maintains an HIV-AIDS surveillance system. Don, a white male representing HELP, said that HELP needed more blacks to be trained as AIDS buddies. The Reverend Wright welcomed us and reminded us that he was an old civil rights veteran and open to helping all people. Jim, the president of the NAACP, said that his organization was ready to respond to the social, cultural, and health needs and threats to the black community.

As moderator for the evening, I, along with the twenty-nine others, was impressed with Fannie and her family's candor about the fear, frustration, and discrimination they faced during David's illness. I also shared the frustration of the health professionals due to the small number of persons present despite all of the effort expended for their public forum. However, the anger, fear, frustration, and frank sharing of thoughts and feelings on AIDS and its consequences were instrumental in drawing this group of thirty persons closer together.

Fourteen black females, eleven black males, four white females, and one white male attended. Eleven of the blacks were members of Fannie's family. All of the whites, except Martha, were from HELP. The evaluation forms revealed that friends, relatives, work associates, and the newspaper were the sources of information about this meeting, not the ministers or the churches. Everyone felt that the meeting was helpful, and they were all interested in providing AIDS education and support to other black East Tennesseans. It was agreed to form a committee to continue the struggle to reach blacks in Happy Valley.

Betty returned to her business activities. Joan, like Dr. Sims, left the valley for a job in the North. The committee of those still interested met at the Red Cross building. Mary, from the County Health Department, was present. Martha was absent but sent Jane, a black nurse, to represent the Red Cross. Doris, from HELP, was absent but asked Sheila, a black nurse, to represent HELP on this committee. Jim, president of the NAACP, joined the committee and asked Dr. Thomas, a newly arrived, black clinical psychologist, to join the committee. As a result, this new committee was all black, as whites who had participated in several joint ventures with blacks were burnt-out or of the opinion that blacks could best deal with AIDS in the black community. This committee, on NAACP letterhead, invited 162 area social, cultural, and religious organizations to send one member of their organization to learn the facts about AIDS and blacks. We received eight replies, but not one member from any of those organizations has met with us.

Lessons Drawn from the Four Events

Blacks in Happy Valley are not yet ready to deal with AIDS prevention: AIDS is not perceived as a problem. What can we learn from these community experiences? Arensberg and Kimball (1972) remind us that community is a process of events measuring historic sociocultural relationships in spatial settings. Any attempt to interpret the activities described concerning AIDS prevention education must be viewed in terms of the regional, class, racial, and gender patterns.

REGIONAL PATTERNS

Happy Valley is situated in East Tennessee, an area noted as the poorest and least politically influential of Tennessee's three major metropolitan regions and the home of the Tennessee Valley Authority (TVA). Its residents, East Tennesseans, and politicians have considered it a region apart. Unlike the traditional South—steeped in indigo, tobacco, and cotton cultivation—East Tennessee is an area of hills, rivers, and valleys lending itself during the antebellum period to household slavery rather than plantation slavery. Intimate relations between blacks and whites led to a patronage such that whites provided theaters, schools, and businesses for their ex-slaves and household servants in the 1920s and 1930s. Local white business leaders' decision to industrialize with light industry (for example, textile, knitting, and flour companies) rather than heavy industry meant that they maintained control of area economic development and race relations. They prevented blacks from garnering the health and welfare benefits of unionized employment. The light industries are not as unionized as heavy industries. Thus, light industries accommodated the upper-class white leadership by providing jobs for the individualistic, hard-working, white, mountain, lower classes, without jeopardizing local race patterns. Blacks were restricted to ancillary industrial service, supportive lower-wage employment, or traditional barber, beauty, clothes cleaning, grocery store, and funereal services. Thus, union health and welfare benefits were not available to lower-class whites or blacks (Beardsley 1987).

Personalized relationships between blacks and whites and the relative isolation due to hilly terrain, on the one hand, coupled with the reservation of mill industrial employment for poor whites and the confinement of blacks to marginal, menial, and patronage employment, on the other hand, led to relative stability in race relations. An unpublished 1971 race-relations report states that whites seldom had to keep the black man in his place. The black man is kept in his own place by the inferior role taught him from his existence on the edge of East Tennessee society. These personalized relationships prevented the formation of broad-based black leadership in schools, churches, and civic organizations to address black community development, periodic unemployment and underemployment, and health care.

African Americans, having a history of seeking health care during the presence of blood or crisis, and with little or no history of preventive health care (Harrison and Harrison 1971) are at great risk of contracting HIV-AIDS since prevention is the only cure. Local patterns of segregation and few black medical doctors confounded health care efforts. In 1988, the mayor of Happy Valley went to Meharry Medical College to recruit black doctors, as the Valley had only one or two black doctors. The state university graduated its first black student in special education in 1954. This legacy of relatively little higher education has led to a relative stability of uneducated and undereducated area blacks with ministers as spokesmen and leaders.

CLASS PATTERNS

In 1980 blacks comprised 14.6 percent of the city population but only 1.6 percent of the county population. Black median family income was only $13,051, contrasted to $20,476 for whites. Happy Valley College, a historic black college, was never able to attract, educate, and train historic black cohesive local leadership like colleges in Atlanta and Nashville. The college drew most of its students from outside of the local area, and its graduates left the local area due to limited local employment. In the 1980s the area lost more than two thousand textile and apparel related jobs. The TVA job force declined from 53,200 to 26,591 persons. Attracting and retaining black professionals and business personnel is a continuing problem. Between 1983 and 1985 Tennessee grew by eighty thousand persons, yet the state lost six thousand black professionals (Lane 1989:25). Since the origin of Happy Valley in 1791, the black population increases and decreases every few years. It is estimated that there were 560 black professionals in the Happy Valley area in 1987, primarily school teachers, nurses, social workers, ministers, and engineers.

The desegregation of higher education at the state university, the TVA, and areawide federally subsidized energy industrial complex has led to an influx of newly skilled blacks. They learn that "credentials for belonging cannot be earned" (Lane 1989:26). They experience area clanishness and the unwritten code dictating that outsiders are not to be trusted, making it very difficult for blacks to settle in Happy Valley. They experience culture shock relating to native blacks in navigating barriers to job advancement, experiencing institutional racism, and getting services. As a result of such patterns of accommodation and subtle racism, blacks like Dr. Sims and nurse Joan leave the area.

Although professional and business blacks may be more knowledgeable about AIDS and prevention oriented, they may also be more hesitant to get involved in AIDS prevention efforts. First, AIDS involves sexual activity, which is a private act and not a topic for public discussion or display. Second, AIDS involves drug use, which is an illegal activity implying criminality. Third, AIDS also suggests homosexuality, bisexuality, or even womanizing—topics unpleasant, embarrassing, or humiliating. This triple stigma of AIDS, plus necessary association with those of different sexual orientations, may be uncomfortable for professional and business blacks. Teenage pregnancy, the dropout rate, and drugs are problems worthy of their efforts, not AIDS.

RACIAL PATTERNS

In our first community event, blacks and whites were following traditional patterns of accommodation. When the white "community" in Talladega, Alabama, wanted to include the Negroes in the health inventory, the superintendent of Negro schools was contacted (Kimball and Pearsall 1954). When whites wanted to study syphilis in Negroes in Tuskegee, a Negro nurse was employed (Jones 1981). And when the Happy Valley Red Cross wanted to reach the black community, they contacted an official in the Community Action Anti-Poverty Agency, who in turn informed the president of the Ministerial Alliance. The Ministerial Alliance assigned the task of the workshop to the Reverend Able, a newcomer to the area. Martha, a white nurse from the predominantly white west side of town representing the private Red Cross, and Mary, a black social worker from the predominantly black east side of town representing the County Health Department, combined their talents to inform black ministers about AIDS. These professional women were trying to garner the support of these primarily male ministers in order to arrest a growing health crisis. The white male university professor of religious studies was a more creditable source of information and authority as he himself was a minister and the representative of the major intellectual center in the area. The white nurse and the black social worker got the ministers' attention, but the white professor got the ministers' respect. The workshop was received by the ministers as personal information to be used if they should ever have a church member suffering from AIDS. They considered it their role to preach and to counsel if the opportunity presented itself. They did not see a role for themselves in AIDS education or prevention.

The second community event, involving the seminar on Acquired Immunodeficiency Syndrome, is a classic example of personal influence in regional race relations. Fannie, a Happy Valley native, was able to activate her family, pastor, church members, and a prominent member of the white community. She told her daughter to ask her boss, Dr. White, to appear on her program. Dr. White told me that he was very busy and did not know if he could stay for the entire program, but he ended up staying for refreshments. This reflects the traditional intimate personal relationships between valley whites and blacks. This also reflects the traditional southern pattern of whites looking out for "their Negroes" on one hand, and monitoring "Negro" activities on the other hand. Attendance was the largest of all community events because this was Fannie's seminar, an event reflecting local personal influence, her network.

The third community activity, celebrating World AIDS Day, reflects the failure of several organizations to sponsor a program sufficiently attractive to interest area blacks. Although the location of the event was a black church, all other sponsoring and supporting agencies were imported from outside of the black community. Fannie was the only native Happy Valleyan on the program, and she permitted herself to be surrounded by health and government personnel: the seminar had been "her thing," but here at the forum she is being a team player.

The lack of participation by other churches in the Ministerial Alliance reflects their lack of teamwork. Although ministers are members of the alliance, they are not necessarily friends. Membership in the alliance does not guarantee unity and cohesion. Most black churches in the valley are results of splinter groups from earlier churches. Most black ministers are nonnatives—neither Able, Goodman, nor Wright are natives. Some ministers are not only nonnatives but also do not reside in the neighborhoods in which their churches are situated. As a result, ministers are often strangers to each other. Between December 1989 and March 1990, two ministers allegedly were "run off" by their congregations. Three of the most popular churches lack full-time pastors. The Reverend Able, when pressed by me to explain the lack of support for AIDS education, told me that most black ministers can't discuss AIDS because its a "no, no"! They can't deal with it. I can deal with it because I am a health professional. A native female senior citizen says some of the ministers wouldn't deal with it because they are "womanizers." A middle-age female native said: "Well, you know it deals with sex and sin and homosexuality, and there are some of them in a lot of church choirs. And one or two ministers are that way." So, if Happy Valley ministers lead, they march to their congregations' tunes. Apparently they have not received their marching orders for AIDS education.

Finally, the NAACP's public forum reflects the traditional role of the NAACP to bring whites and blacks together for a cause necessary for better human relations. It brought more whites and blacks together than any other meeting. The forum had enough potential to attract the state-wide minority AIDS coordinator from the state capital. It gave Fannie and her family an opportunity to go public in their grief and in their attempts to be a source of solace for black families suffering with AIDS. It gave David's lover an opportunity to confront his former lover's family and work out some of his grief and bitterness. It gave HELP an opportunity to try to recruit blacks. It gave the state's minority AIDS coordinator an opportunity to see this part of the state deal with AIDS. It was the matrix for the creation of a technical committee whose purpose is to continue to find the handle to educate the black community in AIDS prevention education.

GENDER PATTERNS

Finally, the role of women must be recognized. Martha, the white Red Cross nurse, was the enabler working between the black community and the white community. She related well with the black females in that she was female and a nurse: Sheila, Jane, and Joan are female and nurses. She related to Mary, Pearl, and Dr. Sims because they were female and public health educators. She related well with the Reverend Able because he and Martha's husband were similar health professionals. Thus, Martha was a central person in articulating information and resources on AIDS to blacks. She recruited the Reverend Able to serve on the Red Cross Board of Directors. It was important that blacks know about AIDS and that the Red Cross had what blacks needed. This was Martha's mission.

However, the role of black women must be highlighted, for they are carrying on in a tradition of health education like earlier black health workers such as Lugenia Hope of Atlanta, Georgia, and Modjeska Simkins of Columbia, South Carolina. Both of these women were very active in public health education campaigns and programs during the tuberculosis and venereal disease epidemics of the 1920s (Beardsley 1987).

The Happy Valley black women are sustaining the local AIDS prevention education among blacks. Except for Fannie and Betty, all are health professionals. Dr. Sims is a public health physician; Mary is a medical social worker; Pearl is a wellness director; and Sheila, Joan, and Jane are nurses. All knew persons with AIDS and all understand the epidemiology of AIDS among blacks.

Four of these women are married with children and are sensitive to the problem AIDS poses for families. On 1 January 1990, the state program director for AIDS surveillance and sero-prevalence announced that 27 percent of AIDS cases are between 20 and 29 years of age, which is higher than the national average of 20 percent. This means that the virus was contracted in the teen years. Use of cocaine and marijuana by Happy Valley County seventh, ninth, and eleventh graders exceeded the national average use for similar grades in the 1988–89 school year. Forty percent of those youth surveyed use alcohol as the drug of choice. Alcohol and drug use can be a risk factor in the transmission of the AIDS virus (Stall 1987; MacGregor 1988; Molgaad et al. 1988). One nurse has a son who is recovering from a severe drug problem. Fannie's brother died of AIDS and hers is the only family to have experienced AIDS directly. Two of the three single women have a child and are sensitive to the possibility of AIDS in children and in the heterosexual population.

Furthermore, all females, except Dr. Sims, Joan, and Pearl, are natives. Thus, their concern and commitment is the protection of their families, friends, and hometown. This is especially true in Happy Valley, where 113 of 200 persons arrested in drug-related activity during the last two years were black. The youngest person was 18 years old, while the oldest was only 41 years old. The majority of persons arrested were in their twenties and thirties. Marijuana is a cash crop, and drug traffic is brisk in the area. For local black women, participation in AIDS prevention education is a life-saving activity bordering on self-preservation and love for their region.

Furthermore, these women are active church women. Although their church leadership may not be as visible as that of their male ministers, it plays a prominent educational role in their churches. These skills are utilized in community AIDS prevention activity as a mission in Christian witness. Thus, the black church continues to be a training ground for women as women continue the tradition of using the church as an alternative structure for influence (Gilkes 1990). Their support roles in the community supplement their educational roles in their churches and are reflected in their professional roles of nurse and welfare worker, extensions of their domestic roles as sisters and mothers (Lewis 1990).

The participation of native females raises the question, where are the native males? This issue needs further exploration and has to be addressed if efforts are to be successful. More males must become involved in community AIDS education.

CONCLUSION

How does a black community organize itself to deal with the AIDS epidemic? In Happy Valley, black female natives form a core, black ministers are on the periphery, while the larger community is not involved. What is needed to increase Happy Valley's consciousness for AIDS prevention education? Three things: more deaths from AIDS; the expansion of female networks to include personnel in public housing areas, and influential among the homeless, street, drug, and gay people; and the movement of black ministers from the periphery to the core for communitywide leadership.

NOTES

1. I want to thank Rosa Emory and Faye Harrison for their comments on an earlier version of this paper.
2. All names are pseudonyms.
3. The school system had no uniform policy for AIDS education. The State of Tennessee was in the process of preparing a policy on AIDS education. Also, a neighboring county school system became embroiled in a confrontation between students and parents over an AIDS patient. Parents wanted to withdraw their children or have the student with AIDS withdrawn from school. Students sided with the AIDS student, against the parents. School officials were caught in the middle with no school policy. AIDS is "too hot to handle," except on an ad hoc basis, at the discretion of the school and the teachers.
4. Crohn's disease is regional ileitis.

In Search of Soul Food and Meaning: Culture, Food, and Health

Tony L. Whitehead

The morbidity and mortality rates from hypertension, heart disease and stroke, and rectal and stomach cancers in the United States are higher among African Americans than among the European American population (National Center for Health Statistics 1982). Many epidemiological and nutritional studies have linked the disproportionate prevalence of these health problems among African Americans to the foods they eat (Todhunter 1976; Hutton and Hayes-Davis 1983), particularly in the South, where the diseases are common and many African Americans continue to practice so-called risky foodways: eating foods high in fat, salt, sugar, and cholesterol.

This paper argues, however, that current research ultimately fails to pinpoint African American foodways as the primary culprit in these health problems. For one thing, no one has yet demonstrated a difference between the foodways of African Americans and European Americans in the South that was then correlated with differences in the prevalence of the chronic conditions mentioned earlier. Without this kind of research design, how can any study conclude a relationship between specifically African American dietary styles and a prevalence of food-related health conditions?

In addition, the sociocultural context of food-related behavior is too often ignored. Current research among African Americans tells us what people eat, how much they eat, and what the biological consequences are, but not *why* people eat what they eat. The latter question is crucial to our understanding of health as it relates to food.

For example, I observed a number of contradictions during my six years of food-related research (1977–83) in Bakers County, North Carolina (a fictitious name). One contradiction concerned the frequency with which primary food preparers in the many households with at least one hypertensive member would *explicitly* tell me how their favored foods and preparation styles put members at risk, even while they continued in such foodways. Other times, the same people who said they didn't eat pork would invite me to a pig-picking (roasting of a pig on a grill) (Whitehead 1984). Such contradictions were examples of what Berreman (1962) calls "impression management." Because of human subject review requirements, we told people from the start that our research focused on hypertension control. For African Americans in the South, particularly in this part of the "stroke belt," [1] high blood pressure is part of the traditional folk epidemiology, as is the belief among some persons that pork is bad for you. Because people didn't want those "doctors from the University of North Carolina" (where I was working at the time) to think they were dumb or self-destructive, some of our respondents "managed an impression" of "correct behavior" by denying the consumption of what we later learned was a favorite food. At the same time, inviting people to a feast (the pig-picking) is part of southern hospitality as well as a way to diminish an outsider's unfamiliarity and social distance. Clearly, these seeming contradictions between knowledge and behavior stemmed from a larger sociocultural system, of which food behavior was a part.

The present paper explores this food-related sociocultural system. A broader argument is also made that the primary problem in foodways research in general, and African American foodways research in particular, is the lack of comprehensive, multidisciplinary approaches that consider the cultural meaning of food as well as its biomedical consequences. Such an approach is presented for effectively studying the foodways of African Americans, southerners, or of any other cultural group: The Cultural Systems Paradigm (CSP), a model that emerged from the Bakers County data (Whitehead 1984).

The CSP (see Figure 1) is an ecological model that emphasizes the sociocultural context of historical process. It is based on a similar model by Jerome and her colleagues (1980b), de Garine (1971), and to a lesser extent Harris (1985). The ecological approach of the CSP uses Ford's (1978:15) notion of culture as a "historical product of environmental adaptation." Stated in another way, culture is part of a larger ecological system, which is historically created, intergenerationally reproduced and moderated, and *functions to allow humans to meet basic biological*

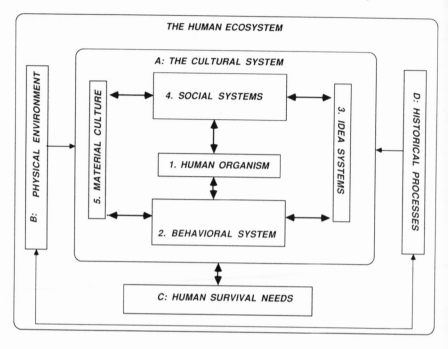

Figure 1
The Cultural Systems Paradigm

and cultural needs in ways that blunt the impact of deleterious environmental agents and exploit agents that sustain life and culture.

In other words, the CSP conceives of culture as helping to fulfill human needs. Because of this, it has been criticized as being functionalist, a theoretical approach that is a throwback to an earlier tradition in anthropology (Malinowski 1944; Radcliffe-Brown 1965). While I resist labels, I have found this tradition helpful in understanding cultural persistence and diversity, particularly because of its concept of holism. Western public health professionals tend to view certain behaviors and ideas among their clients as dysfunctional, and therefore needing change. Such interpretations are usually not based on a holistic analysis, and as such, they fail to see the possible functional roles the behaviors in question might play or how changing single behaviors might have a negative impact on the larger cultural system. Based on the findings from our two data sets from Bakers County and New

Hanover County, North Carolina, I propose that a major contribution to the persistence of cultural traditions, including foodways, is the role such traditions play in meeting needs—sociocultural, psychological, and biological.

In the CSP, culture consists of four primary subsystems: *ideational, social, behavioral,* and *material.* With regard to food-related behavior, the CSP identifies several categories of activities: acquisition, preparation, preservation, distribution, and consumption. Each of these categories has a range of possible sociocultural characteristics, including content, method, participation, routinization, and location. That is, the CSP helps us understand food behavior as part of a cultural system by allowing us to note *what* the food is (content) and who is participating in its use, as well as how (participation and method), when and with what regularity (routinization), and where (location) a group's, household's, or individual's food is acquired, prepared, preserved, distributed, and consumed. These categorizations help us isolate and target that food-related activity which is the unit of analysis.

There are several reasons why a cultural ecological approach is most suited for exploring African American foodways. First and most important, the approach reminds us that culture is a dynamic, continually changing process. With regard to African Americans, it helps to remember that not even plantation slavery could abolish all remnants of the many African cultures. After freedom was gained, heavy postbellum migration by African Americans contributed to new forms of intraethnic American cultural diversity. Moreover, since the 1960s, African American culture in the South has been greatly influenced by the massive return migration of "northern influenced" blacks, as well as by the infusion of nationally based industrial and communication industries, including the highly influential food marketing and advertising industry. Within this dynamic and fluid southern culture, however, Gwaltney (1980) proposes a "core African American culture," which I suspect also includes a specifically African American core foodways system.

In the remainder of this paper, the CSP will be used to explore this core system of African American foodways in the South, and to explore the *institutionalizing* and *regenerative* historical processes that have kept this core food system alive.

"SOUL FOOD" VERSUS SOUTHERN FOODWAYS

The emergence of the idea of soul food during the intense cultural revitalization of African Americans in the 1960s suggested an exclusive ethnic dietary system. Soul food is a reference not only to the *content* of the southern African American diet, but also to its *preparation styles*. Pork is a favorite soul food meat that must be fixed in a certain way. In addition, soul food requires the use of pork fat ("fatback," salt pork, streak-o-lean) as a seasoning in the cooking of vegetables in a slow, stewing manner (vegetables such as collard and turnip greens, black-eyed and field peas, green and lima beans), and in the frying of other favorite foods such as chicken, fish, and potatoes.

The soul food diet also includes various uses of corn and sweet potatoes (including cornbread, grits, hominy, and sweet potato pudding and pie). Corn is frequently the base of numerous quick breads, "hush puppies" (fried cornbread dough), johnnycake, dodgers, and hoecakes and is used in the frying of a traditional favorite: fish. During the 1960s, older African Americans of southern roots would include various wild game in the soul food menu, such as squirrel, rabbit, possum, and deer (Blanks 1984).

African Americans in the South have traditionally favored foods that were prepared with high contents of sugar or salt; as well as those that were "spiced up" with hot peppers; sauces such as tabasco; and spices such as mace, allspice, sesame seed (called "beene"), and "file" powder, made from sassafras leaves. Northerners often remark that southerners tend to prefer overly sweet desserts and summer drinks (lemonade, Quill-Aid, iced tea). Indeed we observed drinks being made with seven to eight cups of water and as much as one and one-quarter cups of sugar. The southern households that my students and I studied also seemed to prefer more salt in their pork (for example, cured country ham), and sweeter, saltier, and hotter spices in their favorite barbecue sauces (for pork and chicken), crab or salmon cakes, and in their jambalaya, gumbo, and other stews, than the northerners we tested.[2]

But are these foods an ethnic creation of African Americans or simply the historical cuisine of a regional people—that is, those residing in the southeastern United States? I am sure that many readers of European origin in the South will quickly reflect that many of the food items and preparation styles mentioned here are not solely those of southern African Americans, but were very much a part of the diet of their own households while growing up. And any person of Cherokee or other southeastern Native American ancestry might view the wild game or corn products mentioned earlier as Indian not African American.

Such repudiations only suggest that the American "melting pot" theory has no better proof than in food. Indeed, it is in foodways, particularly in the South, that we see the mixture of three cultural areas (European, African, and Native American), which gave rise to new food forms such as "spoonbread." According to Neal (1985:5), spoonbread is based on the Native American staple of corn, the soufflé technique of the European, and the African preparation style of mixing technique and ingredient. However, as Abrahams (1984:32) has pointed out, we lack research that systematically demonstrates how, within a few generations, these three groups "developed a unique creole culture" that included new foodways.

Just as one may question whether a distinctly African American diet exists, so too has the existence of a truly "southern" diet been challenged (Fitzgerald 1979). Fitzgerald's conclusion that there is no such thing as southern foodways was, I believe, based on faulty methodology.[3] Moreover, he too-narrowly focused on the content of the diet while ignoring the significance of what it means to southerners to be southern and the important ways in which foodways help support this ideation. For example, spoonbread is southern, because of its complete acceptance by the southern community and its general recognition as a southern food. Thus, says Neal (1985:5), a hot dog is not thought of as German but rather as "thoroughly American, despite . . . its origin . . . [while] pizza . . . is still considered Italian [and] . . . a foreign food," although it "is more widely consumed."

The point is that the content, ethnic origin, preparation styles, and differential consumption of food are less important to our understanding of a cultural group's foodways than is the "meaning" of such foodways to these groups. Just as ethnic or regional identity (that is, being southern or African American) is a cognitive construct, so too is ethnic foodway a symbolism, a state of mind. A food is southern because southerners and others recognize it as such. African American foodways are African American because African Americans recognize them to be so.

A major premise in anthropology is that the key to understanding a people's culture lies in the discovery of meaning (Geertz 1973). Earlier studies of southern foodways—and the foodways of the South's ethnic populations—worked from this premise. But this approach ended with research conducted in the 1940s by Cussler and de Give (1953). Their work and that of other early foodways researchers in the 1930s and 1940s was supported by government programs concerned with economic marginality and its sequelae, including nutritional deficits.

A resurgence of food-related research in the South emerged during the 1960s with the government's War on Poverty programs. But then the trend was the correlational types of studies mentioned earlier, which paid little attention to cultural context, or to the context of meaning. Because meaning is contextual, the understanding of meaning necessitates the study of culture as a system. As such, when food and food behavior take on meaning, as they do for all peoples, foodways become a part of a cultural system (Whitehead 1984).

THE FOODWAYS OF SOUTHERN BLACKS AS PART OF A DYNAMIC CULTURAL SYSTEM

In terms of dietary content my students and I proposed the foods in Table 1 as among the historical "core" foods in the southern African American cultural system (Blanks 1984; Whitehead 1984; Wright 1986). This list was gleaned from my own six years of research in Bakers County, North Carolina, Dr. Delilah Blanks's three-generational study in New Hanover County, North Carolina, and a thorough review of the literature. The Bakers County study included twenty African American and twenty European American households (Whitehead 1984); while the New Hanover County study included thirty three-generational African American family clusters. We also documented that the primary preparation styles included (1) the frying of most meat in pork fat or some other fat; (2) the stewing of vegetables with pork fat added for seasoning; (3) the frying of cornbread, usually in pork fat; and (4) preparation of desserts and drinks with the excessive sugar mentioned earlier.

We also found that although most foods were now acquired from nationally based food outlets (grocery and fast-food chains), many of the forty households studied in Bakers County and the thirty three-generational family clusters studied in New Hanover County continued (1) to garden, or belong to kin/friend networks that garden; (2) to be involved in kin/friend networks that killed hogs and shared various pork products with network members; and (3) to buy fresh produce from roadside stands and from truck farmers who periodically drove through the neighborhood selling their produce.

Women most often turned out to be the "key kitchen people" responsible for buying, preparing, preserving, and dispensing food, and for postmeal cleanup. We found that Bakers County foodways met communal needs in four different settings: (1) the "meal," a sit-down affair with others present; (2) the "petite feast" (our definition), exemplified in the single domestic unit as the pre-church breakfast; (3) the "small feast," which includes the domestic unit members and a small number of network members (for example, adult children and their families or special guests such as the itinerant preacher), exemplified in the post-church dinner; and (4) the "grand feast," such as a family reunion or church homecoming feast attended by extended network members.

What we are calling a core African American dietary content (Table 1) can rarely be seen today in its pure form. These foods have a historical genesis and prevalence, as do the complementary sociocultural foodway patterns described in the preceding two paragraphs. Historically, African American foodways are products of:

1. African foods brought by the slave ships and foods and other components of the African foodways created by the African servants.
2. Sociocultural processes that resulted in the integration of African, European, and Native American foodway systems.
3. A rural physical environment that has long supported traditional African and European foods now a part of the southern food system.
4. Persistent economic and political marginality for African Americans.
5. The emergence of social, ideational, and organic (taste) preferences for patterns related to traditional southern foodways.
6. The universal tendency for foodways to meet other human needs other than mere nutrition.

Table 1

A Nonexhaustive List of Traditional Black Core, General Traditional, and Nontraditional Foods in the Southeastern United States

Traditional Black Core Foods	Traditional Foods External to the Black Core	Nontraditional Foods Now Present in the South
pig tails/ears/feet/ heads/backs	bacon/sausage	processed and canned meats, fish
neckbones	ham/ribs/chops/loins, roast/shoulder	hot dogs
heads/backbones	chicken breast/legs	hamburgers
liver	nonfish seafood	cole slaw
kidney	beef/steak/roast	noodles, macaroni, spaghetti
brains	raw apples/peaches	doughnuts
chiterlings	bananas	honeybuns
hamhocks	oranges	instant cereals
fatback/salt pork/ sidemeat	lemons	prepackaged biscuits/ rolls/cornbread
chicken wings/necks/ backs/feet	cheese	soups
wild game	cookies	applesauce
fish	fish	grapefruit
eggs	raw tomatoes	margarine
collard/mustard/ turnip greens	beef stew	chocolate milk
cabbages	honey	fruit juice
okra	lettuce	white bread
peas and beans	pickles	carbonated beverages
sweet potatoes	butter	
white potatoes		
corn		
poke salad		
cornbread		
biscuits		
pies/cakes/cookies		
rice		
grits		
whole milk		
buttermilk		
coffee		
tea		
onions		
molasses		
jelly/jams/preserves		

Each of the traditionally southern ethnic groups (African, European, and Native American) made significant contributions to what Neal (1985) considers to be southern food. Indeed, when the Europeans arrived in the New World, they quickly incorporated the Native Americans' dietary content and methods of food acquisition—that is, growing or gathering of corn, pumpkins, squash, beans, sassafras, wild plants, berries, and nuts; fishing; and hunting of wild game and birds, including turkeys, deer, racoons, and squirrels. The Europeans contributed domestic animals to the diet, including dairy cattle, swine, and chicken. The Europeans also provided the transportation through which crops such as peanuts, white and sweet potatoes, and lima beans moved from South and Central America to North America and through which gumbo, rice, field peas, bene, sorghum, watermelon, bananas, okra, black-eyed peas, yams, and collard greens were brought—along with slaves—from Africa (Edgerton 1987).

Foods from Europe and Africa became part of the southern food system in part because the rich semitropical ecozone of the Plantation South supported local production (Gibbs et al. 1980). The Triangle Slave Trade between Africa, the Americas, and Europe also supported the amalgamation of the three existing food systems and established the two major southern ports of Charleston and New Orleans as the places where the new foodways reached their zenith (Neal 1985:5).

Yet even though foods from all three cultural areas became part of the staple diet of the three traditional groups, the foodways of the African Americans began to take on a unique patterning because of their slave status. In fact, I would hypothesize that the amalgamation of the different ethnic foodways was possibly greater among the African Americans than the other two groups because of the peculiar way the former *acquired* their food. Slaves acquired some of their food from their masters, including dried beef, pork, and fish imported into the area. By being part of the plantation system, slaves had greater access to certain foods than did Indians or poor whites living outside the plantation. But like the Indians and poor whites, slaves also depended more heavily than members of the planter class on gardening, hunting, and fishing to supplement their meager diet.

It was in the preparation of food that African Americans made the greatest contribution according to accounts of early southern foodways (for example, Edgerton 1987; Hilliard 1972; Joyner 1972; Neal 1985; Taylor 1982; Walter 1971). During the antebellum period, the slave cook was the primary food preparer for both the African American slaves and the European American planter families. According to Edgerton (1987:15–16), "The kitchen was one of the few places where their [slave cooks'] imagination and skill could have free rein and full expression, and there they often excelled." The preference for "spicy" flavored foods was most likely the creation of the slave cook, as she had to find ways to turn the lowly food items given the slave into the culinary masterpieces that some now call southern cooking (see, for example, Edgerton 1987:16).

Excess fat, snouts, tails, ears, and intestines were the least desirable parts of the pig, and the slave cook turned them into tasty delicacies. Pork fat was not only good for frying and seasoning other foods, but its high salt content made it quite tasty. Moreover, for the agricultural worker, pork fat was a source of needed energy for the difficult work of the fields.

The plantation ecology was a primary contributor to food preservation and preparation styles and to the development of certain taste preferences and consumption styles. Dried beef and pork were eaten and pork was smoked in a salt brine, which probably contributed to the relatively higher salt preference shown by southern African Americans today (see note 2). Pork fat and high salt consumption probably were also biologically adaptive to the long hours of work in the plantation fields.

The plantation social system most likely was the primary contributor to the excessive sugar preference in desserts and beverages that we mentioned earlier. Historically, when sugar was first brought to the West from the Orient, the rare delicacy was only available to the well-to-do. However, once it became plentiful through its mass production in the Caribbean and the American South, sugar also became a preference for the masses (Sangster 1973). Moreover, sugar may also have been adaptive to plantation labor productivity as it became a source of quick energy crucial to the otherwise poorly fed agricultural workers.

Although slavery formally ended for African Americans in 1863, the political economy of the plantation system did not. Mainstream white society did everything it could, legally and illegally, to maintain antebellum structural relationships between blacks and whites. Land lease laws and Jim Crow laws, sharecropping forms of agriculture, acts of terror, and other means were used to keep whites politically and economically in power and blacks in a persistent state of poverty and exploitation.

This ongoing plantation-style political economy maintained the marginal status of the African American well past the first half of the twentieth century; similarly, African American foodways continued, particularly the modes of food acquisition. Gardening, hunting, and fishing continued to be significant forms of food procurement (Cussler and de Give 1953). Blacks still got some of their food from "the white man," but now they had to pay cash for it or receive it on credit. For the sharecropping family or the African American small farmer, this frequently meant turning over a good portion of the small pay they received when they, or the white farmer for whom they worked, had a good crop. The continuation of the plantation social system not only helped to entrench the methods of food *acquisition* and the *content* of what was acquired, prepared, preserved, and consumed, but it also helped determine *who* participated in food-related activities and *how* they participated.

Another pattern that I believe has its roots in the plantation system or earlier is the large midday meal with leftovers being consumed in the evening and the following morning. While such patterns can still be found in African and European societies, it is its functional quality within the agricultural system that I think has made it a core African American foodway pattern. Within the sharecropping, tenant, and small family farming systems, total family (excluding young children, the very old, and the infirm) work. The key kitchen females returned to the home at midmorning and prepared the large meal. This pattern was still observed among agricultural families in Bakers County and brought back memories of my own childhood sharecropping family meals in rural Southampton County, Virginia, in the 1940s and 1950s.

Among nonagricultural families in Bakers County, the pattern is less evident, except in those cases in which large households have such diversity of individual schedules that the large meal allows for food preparation convenience and consumption scheduling flexibility. The point is that persistent rurality along with continuing economic and political marginality of African Americans in the South supported a continuity of foodway patterns that had became entrenched during slavery.

Those who argue that the modern-day national diffusion of technological, communication, and transportation advances has effectively wiped out a distinctly southern culture (see, for example, Bender 1975; Friedman and Miller 1965; McKinney and Barogue 1971) have mistakenly reduced the concept of culture to simple behavior and ideas that can be completely destroyed by the introduction of powerful new ideas and material culture. Scholars of natural change and architects of planned change[4] continue to document that culture is more powerful than this, and that what frequently occurs is a syncretic, or what I call in the CSP a "regenerated" product, a culture with characteristics of the old and the new.

Such is the case with foodways in the South. Although southerners have adopted new foodways, the old foodways endure, particularly in the form of communal feasts, when social group members come together to reconfirm their group identity. Even the most cosmopolitan southerners enjoy traditional foods at that time, and they, as well as the area's newer residents, frequent southern food restaurants that continue to bring "a taste of the South to your mouth" (Edgerton 1987).

Other factors carried over from the days of slavery that have contributed to the institutionalization of southern foodways in Bakers County have been the county's lower socioeconomic status and the predominant agrarian lifestyle, even into the 1980s. Thus, traditional methods of food acquisition (gardening, maintaining domestic animals, some hunting and fishing) are still being used to supplement new foods that have been brought into the area by national food industries. Both of the counties we studied in North Carolina have experienced rapid urbanization and industrialization in the past three decades, but even so, regenerative processes that maintain components of traditional southern foodways continue.

For example, national supermarket chains do their own assessments of local food preferences in order to stock those foods. Small grocery stores, roadside stands, and farmers markets also sell local products. Indeed, local foods were produced and consumed by some of the domestic units in our studies, and many of those who didn't do their own home production belonged to extraresidential networks that did continue such production. A number of the more cosmopolitan families in our two data sets belonged to networks in which they received fresh garden and pork products from rural network members. There were other urban families who also maintained gardens and two families who even had "a few hogs out back."

Finally, regenerative processes in southern foodways include the manner in which food and foodways are used to meet needs other than nutrition. For example, in terms of economic functioning, the African Americans whom we observed used food in direct economic exchange (for money, goods, and services) or in a kind of transformation in which an invitation to a feast was also an effective way to establish or maintain a network of people now obligated to provide future assistance (Whitehead 1984).

In addition to meeting what I have outlined as organic (nutritional) and instrumental needs, food and foodways also meet expressive needs in Bakers County. As I have discussed (Whitehead 1984), protocol at a domestic or public food event contributes to both gender role socialization (educational) and leadership (governance) needs. The protocol used at a feast also reflects the role of religion in helping to meet the cognitive needs of some residents in Bakers County. We observed such protocols during feasts in the seating and dispensation of privileges to the minister and other church leaders, the selection of the church as the location for many communal feasts, the significance given the presence of church leaders at secular feasts, and the change in activities that occurred when church leaders were present at secular feasts (for example, the avoidance of rock music and alcohol consumption).

This role of the church is quite important. Elsewhere (Whitehead 1989), I have hypothesized that while the church is a most significant institution in the historical tradition of all southerners, it might be more so to African Americans. This hypothesis is not necessarily due to the great significance of religion to the African societies from whence the slaves came as Herskovits (1941) has argued, but due to the total community institution that the church became over time to African Americans. By total community institution, I am referring to the historical role of the African American church in attempting to meet not only expressive (spiritual) needs but also a full range of organic and instrumental needs as well. Indeed the church for African Americans in the South has been the community, an institutional substitute to meet human needs that the wider (white) society/community fails to meet. Perhaps the greatest significance are the communal needs, the need to create a body that establishes culturally desired rules, values, and normative behavior patterns.

Feasts and their accompanying foodways also meet communicative needs by providing the opportunity to share information and communicate to members the structure of their group realities. Finally, communal gatherings provide an opportunity for group members to congregate and reconfirm their sense of corporateness and their bonds of rights and obligations. As with human groups everywhere, the feast is a central component of communal events in Bakers County; feasts meet objective needs by providing the opportunity for reconfirming group identity, as does the very labeling of a food as "southern" or "soul."

Yet while some blacks identified certain foods as "soul," in Bakers County there were lower-income whites who referred to some foods, such as pork neckbones, as "nigger food" (see also Bennett 1943), while higher-income whites referred to them as "poor peoples food" (Whitehead 1984). These are uses of food as symbols of group identity or as symbols of desirable social and moral superiority (see Sahlins 1976).

Traditional African American foodways also seemed to meet certain affective needs among some Bakers County women, who intimated to us that although they knew their food preparation practices (high salt, sugar, fat, and cholesterol content) put them and their families at risk, they were nonetheless proud to be "known for" their "abilities to cook right" in "the old-fashion way" among their family members, fellow church members, and preachers. For these women, the affective needs of personal identity and social status were important and were being met by their food-preparation abilities.

FUTURE RESEARCH NEEDS: SOUL FOOD, SOUTHERN FOOD, AND SOCIOCULTURAL FLEXIBILITY

While some may accept my argument for the existence of a Southern Foodways System, even I am not convinced that I have persuasively argued for the existence of an African American subsystem within this complex. That is because I realize that the research upon which the present paper is based was not carried out with such an objective in mind, and the sample sizes of the two studies (Bakers and New Hanover Counties) were random and too small to adequately demonstrate such an existence. However, I strongly encourage further research on the topic with a larger, more comparative study in which the foodways of African Americans in the South are compared with the European American foodways in the region as well as with those of African Americans in other parts of the country. Such studies should try to establish whether there seems to be a "core" foodways system among African Americans, with attention not only to dietary content, but to other food-related sociocultural patterns as well.

There already exists a plethora of literature that suggests social and cultural expressions among African Americans that differ from those of other Americans. In the present paper, I have explored how some of those patterns that have been discussed by other authors—such as household organization, strong network involvement, the role of the church, and persistent economic and political marginality—may have given rise to differences in foodways. Continuing research in this area would make a significant contribution not only to our understanding of the relationship of culture and food to health and other areas of human well-being, but would also advance our understanding of the concept of culture. But to be effective, such research efforts must utilize holistic or comprehensive research conceptual models, such as the Cultural Systems Paradigm.

NOTES

1. A number of counties within the coastal and piedmont areas of North and South Carolina, Georgia, and northern Florida have been dubbed the "stroke belt" by cardiovascular disease researchers because of the higher prevalence of stroke and other cardiovascular illnesses there than in other areas of the country.

2. We created an instrument to test relative tastes for salt: a liquid with five different amounts of salt calibrated for levels of seasoning in food. The *medium* concentration (#3) was based on a pretest carried out with students at the University of North Carolina, who stated that, on the average, this was the amount of salt they preferred in their food. In Bakers County, the highest concentration (#5) was selected as the amount preferred.

3. The generalization that so-called southern food habits possibly never existed, as implied in the title of Fitzgerald's article, can't be supported by interviews with 82 white and black residents of a small (six hundred persons), middle-class suburb of a southern city.

4. "Planned" change in health intervention is a reference to change brought by such interventions as compared to "natural" change, which occurs without such engineering.

The Socio-Religious Development of the Church of God in Christ

Hans A. Baer

As most black Baptist and Methodist churches toned down the emotional exurberance of their historical predecessors, a wide array of conversionist sects, particularly of the Holiness and Pentecostal varieties, began to emerge in the rural South during the late nineteenth century and, following the turn of the century, in the cities of both the South and the North. These developments apparently prompted Zora Hurston (1981:103) to assert, "The Sanctified Church is a protest against the high-brow tendency in Negro Protestant congregations as the Negroes gain more education and wealth." This essay focuses on the Church of God in Christ (COGIC), the largest of what are often termed "sanctified churches" in the African American community or what scholars refer to as Holiness-Pentecostal sects.

Previous social scientific studies of the Church of God in Christ have focused on selected dimensions of specific congregations, such as ritual behavior (Clark 1937, Boggs 1977, Burns and Smith 1978, Kroll-Smith 1980). Battie (1961) conducted fieldwork on a congregation affiliated with the Ghostite sect (apparently COGIC) in Southern City (apparently Memphis) as part of his examination of the "status personality" of its membership. Anthropologist Melvin Williams (1974) conducted an extensive ethnography of Zion Holiness Church (pseudonym) in the Hill District of Pittsburgh—a congregation affiliated with the Church of Holy Christ (a pseudonym for COGIC) and anthropologist Peter D. Goldsmith (1989) conducted an ethnography of the Harlem COGIC on St. Simons Island on the Georgia Coast.

In contrast to these studies, this essay focuses on the Church of God in Christ at the denominational level. I discuss the development of COGIC from its roots as a Holiness sect in the Mississippi Valley to its transformation into a Pentecostal sect in the wake of the Azusa Street Revival and eventually into a major African American religious organization with its international headquarters in Memphis, Tennessee—a city which its members affectionately refer to as "Jerusalem" or "Mecca." In addition to archival research on COGIC, my study is based on interviews with several high-ranking leaders of COGIC, visits to COGIC congregations in a rural Arkansas town; Memphis; Flint, Michigan; and Akron, Ohio; and attendance at COGIC's Holy Convocation in Memphis.

THE BLACK HOLINESS-PENTECOSTAL MOVEMENT AS A RESPONSE TO RACISM AND SOCIAL STRATIFICATION

The Black Holiness-Pentecostal sects emerged as responses to changes in the American political economy during the decades following the Civil War, but particularly following the turn of the century. The Holiness movement per se emerged largely as an effort to restore Wesley's doctrine of "entire sanctification" within white Methodism following the Civil War. Although, according to Synan (1971:40), initially the Holiness movement "began as an urban force among the better educated circles" and included "leading figures in the Methodist Church," its most radical wing attracted primarily Methodists and some Baptists in the rural South and Midwest. Most of the major white Holiness sects emerged during the Jim Crow era, and, like Populism, often exhibited racist sentiments. Nevertheless, some black Holiness sects appeared on the periphery of the larger Holiness movement, and occasionally poor whites and blacks joined together for interracial Holiness fellowships. According to Shopshire (1975:40), the first black Holiness sects emerged in the rural areas of the South. While several black Holiness bodies arose out of the African Methodist Episcopal Church and the African Methodist Episcopal Zion Church, most emerged as schisms from Baptist associations and conventions (Shopshire 1975:51).

As changes in agriculture forced blacks to leave tenant farming, sharecropping, and even independent farming, they often accepted menial jobs as unskilled and semiskilled laborers and domestics in nearby towns and small cities. In many other instances, however, they migrated to obtain similar occupations in faraway cities in the North or the West or the large urban areas of the South. Following the "culture shock" hypothesis developed by Holt (1940), several social scientists have interpreted the black Holiness-Pentecostal movement as an adjustment to the social disorganization and cultural conflict that many blacks experienced as they became urban dwellers (Jones 1939; Eddy 1952; Frazier 1963). According to Melvin Williams (1974:182), Zion Holiness Church emerged as "one of those social entities created by the stresses and strains of people dislocated from the rural South settling into the urban North."

Testimonies and ecstatic rituals, including shouting and glossolalia, provided members with an emotional release from the frustrations and anxieties that racism and poverty created for them in their everyday lives. As Ira Harrison (1966) observes, "storefront holiness groups and storefront Baptist groups" create a Durkheimian sense of social identity, dignity, and community. Sanctified or Holiness-Pentecostal congregations generally exhibit a familial ethos, either in the real or fictive sense. Furthermore, for many of their adherents, sanctified churches substitute high religious status as "saints" for a humble social status in the larger society. As Williams (1974:157) observes, Zion Holiness Church provides its members not only a "refuge from the world" but also a subculture that "allocates social status, differentiates roles, resolves conflicts, gives meaning, order, and style to its members' lives, and provides for social mobility and social rewards within its confines."

THE DEVELOPMENT OF THE CHURCH OF GOD IN CHRIST

The Early Years

Charles H. Mason and C. P. Jones served as the founders of a black Holiness sect in the Mississippi Valley which eventually evolved into COGIC. Mason—who began his ministry in the Mount Gale Missionary Baptist Church in Preston, Arkansas, and attended Arkansas Baptist College for a few months—underwent sanctification in 1893 and "preached his first sermon in holiness shortly thereafter" (Shopshire 1975:45). He joined C. P. Jones, J. A. Jeter, and W. S. Pleasant in conducting a Holiness-style revival in Jackson, Mississippi, in 1896. After being expelled from the Mount Olive Missionary Baptist Church for preaching "sanctification," Mason and Jones established a church in an old cotton gin in Lexington, Mississippi, which they eventually named the Church of God and shortly thereafter renamed the Church of God in Christ to distinguish it from the white-controlled Church of God. Jones served as the general overseer, Mason as the overseer of Tennessee, and Jeter as the overseer of Arkansas in the new Holiness sect (Church of God in Christ 1973).

The origins of the Pentecostal movement as opposed to its historical predecessor, the Holiness movement, has been the subject of considerable debate. Distinguished church historians Winthrop Hudson (1973:345) and Sydney Ahlstorm (1975:292), as well as many white Pentecostalists, point to events at Charles Fox Parham's Bible school in Topeka, Kansas, in 1901 as the genesis of modern Pentecostalism. Parham's teaching that glossolalia constitutes the only overt evidence of a convert's reception of the Holy Ghost played a significant role in the beginnings of Pentecostalism, the Azusa Street Revival of 1906 to 1909 in Los Angeles under the leadership of William J. Seymour, a black Holiness preacher and former student at Parham's Houston Bible school. But Synan (1971:121) correctly observes, the teachings "acted as the catalytic agent that congealed tongue-speaking into a fully defined doctrine." Due to his role in the Azusa Street Revival, Tinney (1978:213) contends that Seymour was the "father of modern-day Pentecostalism," despite the fact that he is often overlooked "by those who are contemptible of his race."

In early 1907, three COGIC leaders, C. H. Mason, J. A. Jeter, and D. J. Young, received the gift of tongues during their five-week stay at the Azusa Street Mission. Upon returning from the revival, Mason "began holding all night meetings from 7:30 in the evening until 6:30 the following morning in a small frame church on Wellington, and after five successful weeks, even the white Memphis press took notice" (Tucker 1975:90). In addition to witnessing, shouting, glossolalia, healings, and exorcisms, visitors to the revival could "examine the collection of misshapen potatoes and crooked roots, which the elder called examples of the 'mystical wonder of God' " (Tucker 1975:92). When the General Assembly of COGIC withdrew the "right hand" of fellowship from Mason as a result of his advocacy of glossolalia, he called his own General Assembly in Memphis, which elected him the general overseer and chief apostle with absolute authority to establish doctrine, organize auxilaries, and appoint overseers (Church of God in Christ 1973:xxv). Mason's incorporation of the name the "Church of God in Christ" forced the original body headed by C. P. Jones to rename itself the Church of Christ (Holiness) U.S.A. (Cobbins 1966).

The interracial character of the Pentecostal movement began to break down in the years following the Azusa Street Revival. Both prior to and after 1907, C. H. Mason ordained many white ministers of independent congregations because COGIC was one of the few legally incorporated Holiness-Pentecostal bodies in the Mid-South. Rather than making COGIC a "genuinely interracial" body, this practice provided white Pentecostal ministers access to cheap travel on the railways and the right to perform weddings (MacRobert 1988:58). In 1914 COGIC-ordained white ministers formed the Assemblies of God in Hot Springs, Arkansas, at a gathering reportedly addressed by Bishop Mason (Anderson 1979:189). According to Synan (1986:48), Mason "never openly fought the Jim Crow system of racial segregation, but opposed the racial separations among the Pentecostals that came after the halycon days of Azusa Street."

Despite its roots in the rural South, the black Holiness-Pentecostal movement has functioned for some time as an urban phenomenon as well. Memphis, the major metropolis of the Mid-South, has served as COGIC's headquarters since 1907 as well as the site of its annual "Holy Convocation." COGIC has avoided the practice characteristic of many black mainstream denominations of rotating the convention site. An active program of evangelism contributed to COGIC's rapid growth. In 1908, V. M. Baker, a schoolteacher from Pine Bluff, Arkansas, established COGIC congregations in St. Louis and Kansas City, Missouri.

Elder Mason himself carried the holiness doctrine far beyond the mid-South: in 1907, for example, he traveled to Norfolk, Virginia, holding a three-week revival which planted the seed of Pentecost on the east coast. Thus, when blacks began their migration north during the First World War, Church of God in Christ evangelists would travel to them, preaching holiness, telling the simple stories of the Bible, and offering religious joy and warmth not found in the established northern churches. In 1917 COGIC congregations were organized in Pittsburgh, Philadelphia, and Brooklyn. Evangelists were also at work in Harlem, and in 1935 Elder Fletcher opened a storefront church at 137th and Lenox Avenue, placing Mason's message before the largest urban black population in America. (Tucker 1975:95)

During the 1910s and 1920s, COGIC evangelists established congregations in Chicago, Detroit, Dallas, Houston, Fort Worth, Los Angeles, and many other American cities. In the 1920s, COGIC expanded its operations to the West Indies, Central America, and West Africa.

Mason designated the period of November 25 to December 14, at the end of the harvest season, as the time for Holy Convocation. Thousands of the "saints" from the rural areas of the Mississippi Valley combined their attendance at this religious meeting with their annual shopping expeditions to Memphis. Initially, national meetings were held at 392 South Wellington Street. Beginning in 1925, they were held at the National Tabernacle on 958 South 5th Street, until it was destroyed in a fire in 1936. Mason's church on 672 South Lauderdale served as the site of national meetings until the completion in 1945 of Mason Temple, which reportedly had a seating capacity of seventy-five hundred and constituted the "largest conventional hall owned by a black church" (Church of God in Christ 1973:xxx).

Despite the overall tendency of COGIC to eschew political involvement, Mason adopted controversial positions on selected social issues. Like his socialist contemporary, Eugene Debs, Mason was imprisoned for his vocal public opposition to American involvement in World War I. It is important to note, however, that "Mason did recognize the Scriptural injunction to obey those in authority, and gave his endorsement of Liberty Bonds" (Tucker 1975:97–98). Nonetheless, Mason's pacificism and his appeal among the black masses prompted the Federal Bureau of Investigation to keep the chief apostle of COGIC under close surveillance. According to Synan (1986:48), "Like most of the other Pentecostal bodies in the United States, however, the Church of God in Christ softened this stand during World War II because of the apparent evils of facism and Nazism."

The Succession Crisis Following the Death of C. H. Mason

Throughout his long tenure as senior bishop, C. H. Mason "held nearly complete authority in matters of doctrine and polity" (Shopshire 1975:145). In the mid-1950s, Mason created a seven-man Board of Bishops to assist him and to succeed him. After Mason died on 17 November 1961 at the age of 95, the General Assembly elected an additional five men to the board. When the General Assembly elected

O. T. Jones to the position of senior bishop, a dispute arose as to whether so much authority should be concentrated in one individual.

> [The] Church of God in Christ split into at least three groups, all claiming to be true successors to the COGIC name and property. These were in litigation for six years before the courts determined that a constitutional convention should be convened in 1968. It was, amidst brandished pistols; and Mason's son-in-law, J. O. Patterson was elected to succeed to the title of presiding bishop. Patterson's lenient attitude toward defecting ministers and congregations eventually led most to return. (Tinney 1978:258)

The new constitution stipulated that the General Assembly would elect a General Board of Twelve Bishops, including a presiding bishop, for a period of four years. The presiding bishop, as the chief executive officier, in turn selects his first and second assistant presiding bishops from the members of the General Board, appoints all the department heads and national officers, and appoints new bishops.

Fourteen COGIC bishops, however, formed the Church of God in Christ, International, in 1969 in Kansas City, Missouri (Melton 1978: vol. 1, p. 298). In 1982 this body claimed some two hundred thousand members in some three hundred congregations (Jacquet 1985:230). Despite separate ecclesiastical bodies, "congregations from both factions continue to fellowship with each other" (Tinney 1978:250).

DENOMINATIONALIZATION WITH THE CHURCH OF GOD IN CHRIST

Conversionist sects, such as those found within the black Holiness-Pentecostal movement, characteristically adopt an expressive strategy of social action, emphasizing the importance of various behavioral patterns, such as shouting, ecstatic behavior, and speaking in tongues, as outward manifestations of "sanctification." Conversionist sects tend to be "otherworldly" and apolitical and emphasize individual transformation as opposed to social transformation as a strategy for creating a better world. Nevertheless, Wilson (1969:372) argues that conversionist sects, if they manage to survive and grow, are particularly prone to a process of "denominationalization," by which they accommodate themselves to the larger society.

While COGIC still manifests many sectarian features, particularly ones found in rural congregations and urban storefront congregations, it has been undergoing a process of denominationalization in recent decades. COGIC has grown into the largest black Pentecostal body in the world and claimed in 1982 to have 9,982 churches with 3,709,661 members (Jacquet 1985:230). While its membership count undoubtedly is greatly inflated since it has never conducted a systematic census, COGIC, along with three National Baptist denominations and three black Methodist denominations, constitutes one of the seven largest African American religious organizations in the United States.

Like the mainstream denominations in the African American community, COGIC has developed an elaborate politico-religious organization. Shopshire (1975:148) categorizes COGIC's polity as a "episcopal-presbyterian system where bishops have preponderant power and authority, but assemblies, departments, and boards have enough leverage to decide and act on policy matters." Bishop Patterson "stated that the COGIC is too great a church to be tinkered with by inexperienced mechanics. He further indicated that the Church is not a Democracy, but a Theocracy—God speaks to His people through its leaders, and His sheep know His voice" (Church of God in Christ 1985:206).

The General Assembly acts as the supreme legislative and judicial authority of COGIC and meets annually during the Holy Convocation in November as well as in April. Delegates to the General Assembly include members of the General Board, jurisdictional bishops, jurisdictional supervisors of the women's auxilaries, pastors and ordained elders, two district missionaries and one lay delegate for each jurisdictional assembly, and foreign delegates (Robinson n.d.:46). National departments include the Women's Department, the Sunday School Department, the Home and Foreign Missions, the Department of Evangelism and Board of Education, the Board of Publications, and the Department of Public Relations. Each bishop convenes an annual jurisdictional assembly and appoints new pastors and ordains elders. COGIC congregations within the United States are organized into 109 jurisdictions, each of which is presided over by a bishop. States and jurisdictions are grouped into nine "apostolic regions" and a mission territory. A bishop presides as an "apostolic representative" over each of the apostolic regions. Foreign bishops serve under the supervision of the Department of Missions and the missionary bishop.

COGIC maintains its world headquarters in a renovated hotel building in downtown Memphis and operates a publishing board and several educational institutions. In 1970 COGIC established the C. H. Mason Theological Seminary as part of the Interdenominational Theological Center in Atlanta. In part as a result of the closure of Saints Junior College in Lexington, Mississippi, COGIC plans to establish a four-year institution called Saints University in Memphis at some future date.

COGIC congregations range from modest rural churches and urban storefronts to substantial edifaces. Goldsmith (1989:90) reports that some ten to sixty individuals, the overwhelming majority of whom are female, attend the Sunday morning service at the Harlem COGIC on St. Simons. Harlem, whose members work primarily in service and manufacturing occupations, is a "family church," which draws 90 to 95 percent of its more active members from consanguineal and affinal relatives belonging to three extended families spread out over the Brunswick–St. Simons area.

Despite the fact that Zion Holiness Church had been in existence for over fifty years, Williams (1974:48) found that the congregation still catered to poor people whose "incomes do not exceed five thousand dollars a year." At the congregational level, Pentecostal Temple Institutional Church of God in Christ constitutes perhaps the most profound manifestation of the mainstreaming within COGIC. Pentecostal Temple Institutional, located on the edge of downtown Memphis, is housed in an ornate modern structure, which was completed in 1981 at the cost of approximately $4 million (Patterson 1984). While James Oglethrope Patterson, the presiding bishop, served as the senior pastor of the congregation, it was referred to as the "Mother Church" of COGIC. The sanctuary, which is highlighted in "royal blue and colonial" furnishings, seats up to twenty-five hundred people in cushioned pews and has a choir stand with a seating capacity of 250. The Old Temple now serves as a reception, dining, and cafeteria area. In addition to these facilities, the building complex includes the Rushton M. Henley Memorial Chapel (seating capacity of four hundred), a prayer chapel, a courtyard, twenty-four classrooms, a gymnasium, and an office complex. In contrast to the relatively modest socioeconomic composition of most sanctified congregations, including those affiliated with COGIC, Bishop Patterson observed in his sermon during a Sunday morning service in April 1987 that many of his parishioners have been "blessed with nice homes, cars, and diamonds." Despite the presence of many professional people within its ranks, the majority of Pentecostal Temple Institutional's members probably belong to the working class.

Another manifestation of denominationalization in COGIC is a growing interest on the part of some of its pastors, members, and congregations in social reform programs. COGIC provided the headquarters for the sanitation workers strike, which was punctuated by the assassination of Dr. Martin Luther King, Jr., in Memphis in 1968 (Simpson 1978:262).

> Although there is no strong social or political platform from which this pentecostal organization currently acts, a great deal of deference is afforded by its presence and potential in the city of Memphis and other larger urban areas. The growing power and influence of the Church of God in Christ in religious, as well as in social and political affairs, is clearly evident. The Presiding Bishop of this body, J. O. Patterson, has been consistently recognized in recent years as one of the most influential Black persons in America. (Shopshire 1975:104)

Pentecostal Institutional Temple, COGIC's Mother Church, played an instrumental role in the establishment of the Ministers and Christians League, an organization that spearheaded a drive that resulted in a doubling of the black registered voters in Memphis. COGIC ministers have joined National Baptist and African Methodist ministers in campaigning for candidates and distributing political literature. COGIC members have won seats on city councils and in state legislatures and have been appointed to minor executive branch positions in the federal government (Tinney 1978:265). Robert L. Harris, a COGIC pastor, became the first black state legislator in Utah history when he defeated a white Mormon candidate. Samuel Jackson, a COGIC member, served as an assistant secretary of housing and urban development during the 1970s. COGIC bishop F. D. Washington, who regards a strict conversionist stance toward the world as a "mental block," established a job training center and low-income housing project (Hollenweger 1974:17).

CONCLUSION

Since its emergence as a Holiness sect shortly before the turn of the century, the Church of God in Christ has evolved into a major African

American religious body that exhibits both sectarian and denominational features. Historically and to a large extent today, most COGIC congregations have tended to be highly accommodative in that they have emphasized otherworldly concerns and focused upon personal as opposed to social transformation. At the same time, they have exhibited a passive form of resistance in their rejection of mainstream values and aspirations. Goldsmith (1989) maintains that Harlem COGIC and other Holiness-Pentecostal congregations on the Georgia Coast reject the middle-class ideology (which embodies a belief in the possibility of upward social mobility by means of disciplined work and adherence to a concept of "bureaucratic time") espoused in Baptist churches, even those consisting primarily of working-class members. As Diane J. Austin (1981:242) observes: "Religious forms among the poor and oppressed inevitably will have radical implications. To the extent that believers live in and thereby represent their social situation, their religion will pass a moral judgment on that situation." Yet, such movements rarely, if ever, become vehicles of revolutionary change. According to Goldsmith (1989:18):

> Millenialism may not be the pressing business of the Harlem Church, but it is the linch-pin of its ideological structure. Events of an individual's life are ultimately meaningful to the extent that they determine his status in the coming of the new order, that is, whether he will be among the saved or the unsaved. . . . Pentecostal millennialism . . . is an alternative that insists that there is nothing inevitable about the status quo, that in fact what is inevitable is an eventual overturning of present injustices and the establishment of a harmonious new order.

At best, as we see in the case of COGIC congregations, such religious movements adopt a reformist strategy, much like the black mainstream denominations. In this sense, they serve as hegemonic institutions which, while questioning its racist dimensions, accept the overall structure of capitalist America (Baer 1988). The larger and more affluent COGIC congregations, such as Pentecostal Temple Institutional in Memphis, reflect a growing shift within the black Holiness-Pentecostal movement away from traditional concerns with spiritual salvation to an acceptance of bourgeois values of temporal success and material acquisition. Whether the death of J. O. Patterson in December 1989 marks the beginning of a new stage of the development of COGIC, only time will tell. Undoubtedly, progressive, moderate, and conservative camps within COGIC are in the process of jockeying for ecclesiastical power at the present time, while Louis Henry Ford of Chicago serves as the interim presiding bishop of the largest black Holiness-Pentecostal association in the world.

The Southern Origin of Black Judaism

Merrill Singer

In their landmark work, *Black Metropolis*, a study of the African American population of depression-era Chicago, St. Clair Drake and Horace Cayton (1962:381) provide a graphic account of the tremendous religious diversity characteristic of northern ghettos following the Great Migration. In their words:

> If you wander about a bit in Black Metropolis you will note that one of the most striking features of the area is the prevalence of churches, numbering some 500. . . . On many of the business streets in the more run-down areas there are scores of "storefront" churches. To the uninitiated, this plethora of churches is no less baffling than the bewildering variety and the colorful extravagance of the names. Nowhere else in Midwest Metropolis could one find, within a stone's throw of one another, a Hebrew Baptist Church, a Baptized Believers' Holiness Church, a Universal Union Independent, a Church of Love and Faith, a Holy Mt. Zion Methodist Episcopal Independent, and a United Pentecostal Holiness Church.

Further, they note that "among these cults are a few non-Christian groups—the Black Jews, two Temples of Islam, a Temple of Moorish Science, and a small kingdom of Father Divines Peace Mission" (Drake and Cayton 1962:642). Most members of these cultic groups, Drake and Cayton point out, came from the poor and working classes and were drawn especially from migrants from the South. These individuals sought "to recapture the spirit of the 'old-time religion' " (Drake and Cayton 1962:634) they had known prior to their move northward.

In their search for a more satisfying, supportive religious environment, the urbanized African American masses created what Drake and Cayton refer to as the "new Gods of the city" (Drake and Cayton 1962:635). This is an appellation borrowed from Arthur Huff Fauset's (1971) classic account of the self-appointed spiritual leaders and colorful prophets of pre–World War II African American religious cults.

In his important work, *Black Gods of the Metropolis*, Fauset (1971:7) maintains that "with the migration . . . from the rural South to urban centers, a transformation in the basic religious life and attitudes" occurred among African Americans. Following Ira Reid (1940:85), he argues that groups like "Father Divine, Daddy Grace, Moslem sects, congregations of Black Jews and the Coptic Church . . . [were] socially adapted to the sensationalisms and other unique characteristics of city life" in the North rather than traditional agrarian life in the South.

Similarly, E. Franklin Frazier in *The Negro Church in America* (1963: 54) writes: "The 'storefront' church represents an attempt on the part of the migrants, especially from the rural areas of the South, to re-establish a type of church in the urban environment to which they were accustomed. They want a church, first of all, in which they are known as people."

Taken together, these seminal studies paint a definite picture of the origin of heterodox religious tendencies among African Americans. Cut off from their familiar rural occupations and separated from the social networks and cultural patterns of the South, African American migrants in the industrialized metropolises of the urban North turned to the church to provide some semblance of their traditional lifestyle. Accustomed as they were to folk-Christianity with its "informal, demonstrative, preacher-oriented churches" (Spear 1967:175), many migrants were startled by the formal nature of the middle-class African American denominations they encountered in the city. As a result, a "tidal wave" (Reid 1926:276; Landes 1967) of storefront congregations offering familiar patterns of worship and sociability sprang up in the segregated, inner city ghettos of Chicago, New York, Philadelphia, and beyond (but see Nelsen and Nelsen 1975:50). These cults and sects became widespread and plentiful because they offered a mechanism for urban adaptation, stress reduction, peer support, and group survival in the face of social and economic oppression in white urban society.

While there is no denying that the Great Migration gave birth to an array of new African American religious groupings so vast that it has yet to be fully documented, the purpose of this paper is to call into question the solely northern genesis of African American religious sectarianism. Specifically, the paper is concerned with exploring the southern roots of one of the important and intriguing religious types mentioned in the early studies cited above, namely black Judaism. While black Judaism has been most successful and received its greatest attention in several northern cities, and even outside of the U.S. (Brotz 1970; Singer 1982; Singer 1985), its deepest roots can be found in the changing socioeconomic conditions faced by African Americans in the postbellum South.

AFRICAN AMERICANS AND THE BIBLICAL ISRAELITES

Black Judaism is an example of a religious type that Baer and I (Baer and Singer 1981; Baer 1984) have called the *messianic nationalist sect*.

> As the term implies, messianic-nationalism combines religious belief with the ideal of achieving cultural independence and political or even territorial self-determination. . . . Characteristics that stand out as the core features of messianic-nationalism include: (1) acceptance of a belief in a glorious Black history and subsequent "fall" from grace; (2) adoption of various rituals and symbols from established millenarian religious traditions; (3) messianic anticipation of divine retribution against the White oppressor; (4) assertion of Black sovereignty through the development of various nationalist symbols and interest in territorial separation or emigration; and (5) rejection of certain social patterns in the Black community.
> (Baer and Singer 1981:5–6)

Despite their underlying ideological unity, messianic-nationalist sects differ in the source of their particular expression of politico-religious identity and ritual. Contemporary Jewish practice and biblical accounts of the ancient Hebrews provide the fountainhead for the sociocultural patterns found in the various and varied strands of black Judaism. As Landing (1974:51), points out, "The terminology is as varied as their numbers, some referring to themselves as Israelites, others as Jews, Hebrews, Canaanites, Essenes, Judaites, Rechabites, Falashas, and Abyssinians. . . . Although the terminology differs, all such groups perceive themselves as lineal descendants of the Hebrew Patriarchs."

Various writers have suggested that the ultimate roots of black Judaism lie in the identification of African American slaves with the Egyptian servitude and liberation of the biblical Hebrews (Brotz 1970; Shapiro 1970; Singer 1979). Notes Jones (1963:40), "The religious imagery of [African American] Christianity is full of references to the suffering and hopes of the oppressed Jews in Bible times." This natural empathy found its earliest expression in the spiritual music of the slaves (Singer

1985). Above all, it was "the compelling sense of identification with the children of Israel, and the tendency to dwell incessantly upon and to relive the stories of the Old Testament that characterized the religious songs of the slaves" (Levine 1977:23). For example, just prior to Lee's surrender, a white resident of Alabama recorded the words to a spiritual song she heard during a religious gathering among the slaves in her area.

> Where oh where is the good old Daniel,
> Where oh where is the good old Daniel,
> Who was cast in the lions den?
> Safe now in the promised land;
> By and by we'll go home to meet him,
> By and by we'll go home to meet him,
> Way over in the promised land.
> [recorded in Wiley 1938:109]

As Raboteau (1978:250) concludes, through spirituals like this one, "the slaves' identification with the children of Israel took on an immediacy and intensity which would be difficult to exaggerate." Given their respective day-to-day experiences, "songs about Moses and Joshua must have had a much more personal and immediate meaning to the Afro-American than to his white master" (Courlander 1966:42).

Similarly, folk preachers among the slaves were conversant with biblical stories and used them regularly in their sermons. Genovese (1974), for example, records the case of John Jasper, a popular African American preacher from Virginia, who was regularly asked to give his sermon on Joshua to both slaves and whites. Drake and Cayton (1962:623), writing of the period after the migration, note that "a good preacher must 'know The Book.' Among the most popular Bible stories are 'The Prodigal Son,' 'The Three Hebrew Children in the Fiery Furnace,' and 'The Parable of the Virgins,' together with the exploits of Moses, Samson, David, Ester, Solomon, and other Jewish heroes." For some slaves, biblical stories offered a political message in addition to the spiritual comfort they provided. Uya (1971:289) argues that "ambitious slaves saw in the Mosaic tradition an invitation to dress themselves in messianic garments and a justification for revolt against their oppressors." Herein lay the potential of Hebraic identity to furnish a messianic-nationalist response to white oppression. It is noteworthy that slave rebellion leaders like Gabriel Prosser, Denmark Vesey, and Nat Turner all took inspiration from the Bible. Vesey, for example, interpreted several verses from Zechariah and Joshua as heavenly calls to battle against the sin of slavery (Wilmore 1972). Adds Marable (1981:18–19):

> The black faith of a Nat Turner posed a crucial problem for slave culture. If Moses was a deliverer of the Israelites from slaveholders in Egypt, could not a black messiah lead his people from bondage into a new Canaan land? Did not Moses command his children "to wade in the water"? Could not the rebellious acts of a Sojourner Truth or Harriet Tubman be seen in the Bible as Joshua's battle of Jerico, when the walls of the oppressor tumbled to the ground? If the masters were slow to make the connection between the Bible as a text for liberation and the messianic character of servile rebellions, the blacks themselves were sufficiently intelligent to grasp the sanctions for revolt within the Scriptures.

THE EMERGENCE OF BLACK JUDAISM

The exact route of transition from metaphoric, symbolic, or politically coded use of Old Testament figures, place names, and events to express the harsh conditions experienced by the slaves and their hoped for liberation to an actual adoption of Hebraic identity and alleged kinship is historically unclear. Brotz (1970:1), for one, maintains that "as early as 1900, Negro preachers were traveling through the Carolinas preaching the doctrine that the so-called Negroes were really the lost sheep of the House of Israel. There is no reason to think, however, that such reflections did not begin much earlier, in fact during slavery itself, when the more imaginative and daring of the slaves began to wonder about the very human question of who they really were and where they really came from." The source for Brotz's assertion about the message of itinerant preachers in the Carolinas in 1900 is not provided. One intriguing possibility is that their work began during a postbellum South Carolina gubernatorial race. According to Genovese (1974:252), "After the war black preachers took the political stump to tell the freedmen in South Carolina that the Republican gubernatorial candidate, Franklin J. Moses, was none other than the man himself [that is, the biblical Moses], who had come to lead them to the Promised Land." Given the deep intimacy that African Americans during this era commonly felt toward the ancient Hebrews, this confusion of the biblical Moses with his mortal namesake is not hard to understand. Certainly, many African

Americans in the South had been awaiting Moses' arrival since before the Civil War. In fact, some slaves had concluded "that the abolitionists and Union troops were agents of Moses" (Marable 1981:26). Belief in the actual appearance of Moses in South Carolina may well have helped finalize identification with the Children of Israel for some individuals.

At any rate, it is clear that the first efforts to organize distinct black Jewish congregations began just before or after the turn of the century and that they began in the South. Some have suggested that the origin of the earliest black Jewish groups might be traced either to the slaves of Jewish slave owners or to individual African American converts to Judaism prior to the turn of the century. Bertram Korn (1961), who studied African American and Jewish relations in the antebellum South, discounts both of these possibilities based on the limited available evidence. While Korn identifies a number of prominent Jewish slave owners, including Judah P. Benjamin, secretary of state of the Confederacy from New Orleans; Nathan Nathans, president of prestigious Beth Elohim Congregation in Charleston, South Carolina; Maurice Barnett, a New Orleans Slave Block operator; and Benjamin Mordecai, a South Carolina legislator, there is no indication that these men attempted to convert their slaves to Judaism. In fact, in 1820, Nathan Nathans's Beth Elohim Congregation adopted a synagogue constitution that both discouraged conversion efforts and explicitly barred people of color. Although there is record of a number of African American members of southern Jewish congregations prior to and after the Civil War, including at least one member of Beth Elohim in 1857 (Bleich 1972), there is no historic record that any of these individuals attempted to organize distinct black Jewish groups (Berger 1978). Instead, the earliest black Jewish sects were organized by working-class men who, as far as is known, lacked a clear-cut involvement with white Jewish congregations.

THE EARLIEST BLACK JEWISH SECTS

The oldest known black Jewish sect was called the Church of the Living God, the Pillar Ground of Truth for All Nations. Organized by a widely traveled African American seaman and railroad worker named F. S. Cherry, the sect was founded in Chattanooga, Tennessee, in 1886, although little information exists about the church from this period (Shapiro 1970). Cherry later moved the group to Philadelphia, where it was studied by Fauset in the early 1940s. Based on his interviews with the group's leader, Fauset (1971:32) described Cherry as a self-educated man, conversant with Yiddish and Hebrew, who "boasts that he never spent a day of his life in school." In fact, Cherry belittled formal education and challenged educated visitors to his church to disprove any of his pronouncements. In his conversations with Fauset (1971:32), Cherry was also very critical of the South, which he likened to "a place worse than hell."

Cherry taught his followers that in a vision God called him to establish a church and bring to the world the message that the true descendants of the biblical Hebrews were African Americans. Moreover, he insisted that both God and Jesus, as well as Adam and Eve, were black. White people, in his interpretation, were the offspring of the servant Gehazi, who was cursed by the prophet Elisha with skin "as white as snow" (2 Kings 5:27). Moreover, Cherry preached that white Jews were interlopers and frauds (Fauset 1971:34).

In Cherry's cosmology, there are three levels of heaven; the first is inhabited by people, the second is in the sky, and the third is the dwelling place of God. Moreover, he believed that the Earth is square, a doctrine that led members in recent years to discount the authenticity of photographs of the Earth produced by satellites in recent years. Cherry believed that God created the world six thousand years ago and every two thousand years there is a sweeping transition. The first was the Flood experienced by Noah and the second the coming of Jesus. The final dispensation will occur with the return of Christ in the year 2000. Cherry viewed the enslavement of African Americans as punishment for their disobedience to God's commandments as expressed in Deuteronomy 28. During slavery, he claimed, African Americans were systematically stripped of all vestiges of their Hebraic heritage, but in the year 2000 they will once more assume their true identity. The entire history of African Americans, in his view, was preordained. As one of Cherry's followers explained in a letter collected by Fauset (1971:115): "We were brought over here in 1619 as slaves to work for this nation that rules this country and we served 245 years. . . . We were chased out of Palestine by the Romans into the west coast of Africa where we were captured and sold into this great U.S.A. God said we must return to our homeland at a set time."

Cherry urged economic independence for the African American community. Members, particularly men, were encouraged to acquire a trade and to go into business for themselves. Women were taught to specialize in domestic skills. Important in the appeal of the Church of God was its creation of community solidarity among its members. As Fauset (1971:33) observed, the "general atmosphere of the [sect was] like that of a close-knit club or fraternal order."

Based on his observations of group ritual, Fauset describes Cherry's group as having many characteristics of a holiness sect, including rigid rules against drunkenness, secular dancing, taking and exhibiting photographs of oneself, watching television, smoking, swearing, and divorce for any reason, although speaking in tongues and emotional displays, common features of holiness groups, also were condemned. Religious services, following Jewish custom, ran from sundown Friday until sundown Saturday. Fauset (1971:36) observed that several men "who wear uniforms which resemble military dress, and from whose sides swords dangle" were placed around the group's meeting room to service as sergeants-at-arms. The Sabbath ritual consisted of group hymns, discussion of a Bible passage, and a sermon by Cherry, often about the usurpation of Israelite identity by white Jews. Neither Christmas nor Easter was celebrated by the group, but baptism was performed. According to Shapiro (1970), the only traditional Jewish festival observed was Passover meal.

After Cherry's death at the age of ninety-five, leadership passed to the prophet's son, Prince Benjamin F. Cherry. However, group members deny that Cherry ever really died. Rather, they believe that he merely went "where his people could not see him" and "would return in spirit to lead the Church through the person of his son" (Shapiro 1970:139–40). To affirm the founder's continued connection with the church, a recording of one of his sermons is played every Sabbath.

Perhaps the second oldest black Jewish group was called the Church of God and Saints of Christ. William S. Crowdy, a cook on the Santa Fe Railroad, was the founder of this group. Crowdy proclaimed that he was called by God to lead his people back to their historic religion and identity. In 1896, he established his church in Lawrence, Kansas, among former slaves who had fled westward in search of land and freedom from the rising wave of white oppression. Following Cherry's example, Crowdy moved his church to Philadelphia in 1900, but moved again in 1905 to Belleville near Portsmouth in Nansemond County, Virginia, where the group prospered. Branches of the church were established in a number of cities in the United States and overseas as well.

In Crowdy's formulation, African Americans were described as heirs of the ten lost tribes of Israel, while white Jews were seen as the offspring of miscegenation with white Christians. Various Jewish ritual symbols—such as the performance of circumcision on newborn boys, use of the Jewish calendar, wearing of skullcaps, observance of Saturday as the Sabbath, and celebration of Passover, including smearing animal blood on the outside of their homes in honor of God's method for differentiating Jewish from Egyptian homes in the Book of Exodus—were adopted by Crowdy. These were blended with Christian practices, including baptism, consecration of bread and water as the body and blood of Christ, and foot washing, to form a unique ritual synthesis.

Just before World War II, Jones (1939) described a Sabbath service in the Washington, D.C., branch of Crowdy's church, suggesting the absence of traditional Jewish rituals. Members came dressed in uniforms consisting of blue blouses and brown skirts for women and brown suits and bow ties for men. Officers wore metal badges on their lapels. Services began with testimonials, followed by several hymns sung by the choir. A bugle call signaled the beginning of a procession by the choir around the church. This was followed by a sermon. After a lunch break, the service continued until the evening with a presentation by the students in the group's Sunday School and a literary program.

Following Crowdy's death, leadership passed to his hand-picked successor Bishop H. Z. Plummer. Under Plummer, the "chief rabbi" of the group, who was seen by members as a descendent of the biblical Abraham, the group stressed communalism and independent economic development. At its thousand-acre Belleville headquarters, group members lived collectively and operated a farm, several cottage industries, a school, and homes for orphans and the aged. The sect also ran a youth camp in Galestown, Maryland, that served as a referral and rehabilitation center for court-referred youthful offenders. Workers in group-owned businesses were assigned to jobs by an elder of the church. The income they generated was turned over to the church in exchange for weekly rations at the commissary. As Shapiro (1970:117) indicates, emphasis was placed "upon social stability, parental moral responsibility for children, and care for one's own people through social welfare programs." Efforts by Shapiro to update knowledge of current practices in the church were ignored by group leaders in Belleville, who appear to prefer isolation from the wider world. Efforts by Jewish community leaders to convince Plummer to drop Christian practices and undergo formal conversion to Judaism also were rebuffed (Berger 1978).

A final group of note is the Church of God in David. This sect was founded perhaps as early as the 1920s in Alabama. The founder of the group was named Bishop Derks Field. Possibly because of local white hostility, Field moved the church to Detroit. When Field died, a power struggle between two of his brothers and his close associate, W. D. Dickson, lead to a split in the church. Dickson assumed the title of bishop over his portion of the flock and renamed the group the Spiritual Israel Church and its Army. In Dickson's account, he pulled Spiritual Israel "out of David" at the instruction of the Spirit (cited in Baer 1984:27). As "the King of All Israel," a title assumed by Dickson and passed on to his successors, Dickson moved the church to Virginia for a while, only to return it to Michigan "upon further instructions from the Spirit" (Baer 1984:27).

Based on his study of the group, Baer (1984:28) reports: "Members of Spiritual Israel Church view themselves as the spiritual descendants of the ancient Israelites . . . and their organization as a restoration of the religion of the ancient Israelites. In their belief, 'Ethiopian' is the 'nationality' name of Black people whereas 'Israel' is their 'spiritual' name. . . . Furthermore, the first human beings were Black people, starting with Adam, who was created from the 'black soil of Africa.' All of the great Israelite patriarchs and prophets, including Noah, Abraham, Isaac, Solomon, David, and Jesus, were Black men." As for white Jews, the Spiritual Israelites believe most are the descendants of non-Jews who intermarried with the Israelites.

Although Baer (1985) notes the continued use of the Star of David to adorn church buildings and costumes, the group does not appear to have adhered to any specific Jewish rituals or dietary prohibitions. For example, Spiritual Israelites maintain that white Jews practice "circumcision by the flesh" whereas group members practice "circumcision by the heart," which involves "cutting hate from around the heart" (quoted in Baer 1985:109). For the most part, this group adopted beliefs and practices common among syncretic spiritual churches, except that it retained a nationalist tone atypical of most spiritual groups other than the

Universal Hagar's Spiritual Church, which also incorporated black Jewish elements (Baer 1984). Exemplifying this aspect of group ideology is their belief that the founding of their sect represents the "beginning of the deliverance from bondage of white oppression" (Baer 1985:110). Overall, Baer (1985:123) concludes, "The rhetoric of Spiritual Israel tends to be more militant than most black Spiritual groups but more accommodative than most black religious nationalist groups."

As the foregoing account of three of the earliest black Jewish groups reveals, they shared several significant traits. First, all three were either founded in the South or soon established headquarters there. While the northern urban environment may have played an important role in their later development, understanding the emergence of these groups requires an exploration of events and conditions in the South prior to the Great Migration. Second, the beliefs and rituals of all three of these groups represent highly syncretic systems, products of a folk amalgamation of diverse elements. While strong identification with the biblical Israelites, including belief in lineal or spiritual descent from the Patriarchs, was central to the ideology of these groups, this clearly did not preclude the inclusion of numerous non-Jewish practices, including acceptance of Jesus as a messiah figure. Third, messianic nationalism colors the perspective of all three groups. While these sects may not have been especially active publically in protesting racial discrimination and oppression, all three incorporated a strong critique of the wider society and a sense of separation from the secular world. Finally, all of these groups were founded by charismatic prophet figures, "Black Gods" who heard their calling and began to gather their flocks *prior* to arriving in the metropolises of the northern and midwestern states.

SOUTHERN IMPETUS FOR BLACK JUDAISM

What factors, beyond the close African American identification with biblical Hebrews, may have contributed to the emergence of these early black Jewish congregations? Several historical events appear to have played an important role in the sectarian turn toward Judaism. First, there was the response of southern clergy to the emancipation of the slaves. As Shelton Smith (1972) has shown in his history of racism in southern religion, after the Civil War southern ministers clung to the notion that slavery was a divinely inspired practice. Among the Presbyterians, for example, a southern church assembly in Macon, Georgia, just after the war affirmed slavery was supported by "Scripture and reason" (cited in Smith 1972:209). Professors at both Columbia Theological Seminary and Union Theological Seminary continued to publish proslavery articles in the *Southern Presbyterian Review* for many years after the Emancipation. Similarly, Jeremiah Bell Jeter, senior editor of the *Richmond Religious Herald*, the most prominent southern Baptist newspaper, remained an ardent defender of slavery as a righteous institution after the war. His views were shared by other southern Baptist leaders and continued to be voiced on the floor of southern Baptist conventions long after the institution of slavery was abolished. Southern Methodists, too, continued to speak openly in defense of slavery as a divinely sanctioned practice. For example, Thomas O. Summers, editor of the *Nashville Christian Advocate*, and Linus Parker, editor of the *New Orleans Christian Advocate*, were printing proslavery articles well into the 1880s.

What was the net effect of the refusal of southern religious leaders to accept the end of slavery and to extend fellowship to African Americans? Smith (1972:226) notes that by 1866 African Americans "were pouring out of Baptist churches." Similarly, while there were over 170,000 African American Methodists in 1860, by 1866 this figure had fallen to just under seventy-nine thousand (Smith 1972). A parallel development occurred in the Presbyterian church, which lost most of the ten thousand or so African American members it had prior to the Civil War. As these figures suggest, the inability of southern religious leaders to sever their embrace of human bondage and racial oppression led to a mass flight of African Americans out of white dominated Christian churches. Many of these individuals joined newly formed African American Christian denominations. However, for some, southern Christianity's rejection may have led them to consider heterodox alternatives. Thus, Sheppardson and Price (1958:98) point out that in Richmond, Virginia, in the 1890s, there were "a host of . . . less orthodox sects, with their prophets and messiahs, which flourished in the atmosphere of open-air, river baptisms, with their associations of John and the Jordan." At about the same time, a number of cultic groups following one or another self-proclaimed messiah appeared in African American communities of Georgia. One such figure, Dupont Bell, developed a group of adherents in 1899 in the area around Savannah, Georgia, after claiming divine status (Parker 1937). Although Bell lost his disciples after he was committed to an asylum, his ability to attract a following reflects the readiness of southern African Americans during this period to embrace nonmainstream religious options. As Shapiro (1974:255) concludes, "The forces excluding blacks from full participation in society also excluded them from any real participation in the Christian faith as defined and delimited by whites. This exclusion may well have made some black people receptive to other religious traditions and modes of expression."

Second, for the first fifteen years after the Civil War, the southern economy was in a shambles. "Poverty and dilapidation pervaded the countryside and small towns as well. Highways and railroads were in disrepair, stores lacked customers, and the beautiful antebellum homes of the planters were often abandoned and falling in ruins" (Johnson and Campbell 1981:62). Nonetheless, after the war, African Americans "began migrating to southern cities in increasing numbers" from rural areas (Kornweibel 1981:88). Many came to the city "seeking a new life away from the reminders of slavery and plantation agriculture" (Kornweibel 1981:88). Beginning in about 1880, the southern economy began to improve with the influx of northern and British capital. Within a few years, "railroads were built, seaports bustled, tobacco and cotton were in demand, and the iron industry in the South was transformed from a potentiality to a reality" (Johnson and Campbell 1981:62–63). As a result, opportunities for employment began to open up for some African Americans, including jobs on the railroads and merchant ships involved in renewed southern commerce. These jobs provided the opportunity for men like Cherry and Crowdy to acquire diverse experiences and to be exposed to nontraditional ideas and ways of life. These experiences may well have contributed to their adoption of a heterodox route to religious expression.

Third, after the Civil War, a number of prominent African American leaders began urging their followers to use the Jews as a model for overcoming their abundant hardships. Benjamin Tucker Tanner, editor of the leading African American magazine of the day, the *African Methodist Episcopal Church Review*, urged his readership to emulate European Jews who had overcome great adversity to achieve a measure of economic success (Meier 1963). A similar message was offered by

Booker T. Washington (1902:7), who claimed that unless the African American "learns more and more to imitate the Jew . . . he cannot expect to have any high degree of success." Built onto the older identification with biblical Hebrews, the prompting by recognized leaders to model their lives after contemporary Jewry probably helped to strengthen African American interest in Jewish identity.

Fourth, in 1883 the U.S. Supreme Court ruled that the Civil Rights Act of 1875 was unconstitutional and that the federal government could not outlaw racial discrimination by private individuals and groups. The ruling set the tone for a new era. By 1890 Reconstructionism had fallen into disrepute and "race relations were deteriorating throughout the South, in the cities as well as in the countryside" (Kornweibel 1981:91). Black codes and other discriminatory Jim Crow laws were enacted by state legislatures across the South in order to destroy postwar African American political and social participation and to ensure that former slaves "remain a dependent, nonpolitical, and landless laboring class" (Redkey 1969:2). Adding teeth to the new legal and political restrictions, the number of African Americans lynched in the South grew throughout the 1880s and early 1890s, "averaging about 100 a year during the two decades and climbing to a peak of 161 in 1892" (Meier and Rudwick 1970:168). In southern cities, the incidence of racist mob violence also increased during this period. Through these various strategies, "patterns of disenfranchisement, segregation, and racial subordination were brought to completion during the early part of the twentieth century" (Meier and Rudwick 1970:168). This wall of oppression also appears to have been a factor prompting the messianic nationalist turn among African Americans, including the turn toward Judaism, a religion whose white members also were under attack during the racist upsurge. For some African Americans, adoption of a Jewish identity came to serve as a needed "counterpoint to the popularized racism of the Jim Crow South" (Shapiro 1974:259).

Finally, in response to the worsening social conditions in the South, toward the end of the nineteenth century there developed a nationalist upsurge among African Americans. As Edwin Redkey's (1969:22) review of this period indicates, "The collapse of Republican Reconstruction had demoralized many who believed, with much justification, that the violence and economic oppression that had threatened them throughout Reconstruction would soon become intolerable. The discontent that grew from political and economic changes provided fertile soil for black nationalism." The first flames of this nationalist sentiment were kindled in a reborn back-to-Africa movement that swept across South Carolina in 1877. The leadership of this new movement soon was assumed by Bishop Henry M. Turner of the African Methodist Episcopal church, "without doubt the most prominent and outspoken . . . advocate of black emigration in the years between the Civil War and the First World War" (Redkey 1969:24). Turner's numerous fiery speeches at church conventions across the South helped to focus African American discontent and disillusion. Central to Turner's philosophy and later that of most black Jewish groups was the idea that African Americans have as much right biblically and historically to maintain that God is black as do white people who portray Jesus as well as God as white.

Despite abundant oratory skill and tremendous effort, Turner was unable to build a successful emigration movement. Redkey (1969:301) identifies an important reason: "American blacks, cut off from most of their African memories and immersed in a nation that refused to acknowledge that blacks could have a cultural background, have had a difficult time fashioning a cultural identity other than the tradition of oppression. Bishop Turner was unable to find or create a mythical structure of the Afro-American past that would inspire his people." In the Old Testament accounts of the biblical Israelites, men like F. S. Cherry, William Crowdy, and Derks Field found such a mythical charter, which they used to found African American sects that have endured throughout the twentieth century. Included among the offspring of the groups started by these men is the Black Hebrew Israelite Nation, which did succeed in leading several thousand African Americans out of the United States to their current residence in Israel (Singer 1979).

CONCLUSION

In sum, as Wilmore (1972:210) comments, "The period between 1890 and the Second World War was one of luxuriant growth and development for many forms of black religion in the United States." By the end of the 1930s, African American neighborhoods were "literally glutted with churches of every variety and description" (Wilmore 1972:222). Black Judaism, as we have seen, has long formed a small but significant piece of this grand religious mosaic. As one expression of the messianic-nationalist response to white racial domination, black Judaism offered an alternative identity founded on an enduring African American empathy with the suffering and deliverance of the biblical Israelites.

Generally, the social scientific and historic literature that addresses the topic has tended to give the impression that the tremendous religious creativity among African Americans that produced a broad spectrum of religious forms only began after the Great Migration, as rural migrants struggled to find a niche in their strange new urban environment. Brotz (1952:324), in fact, explicitly states that black Jewish groups "were all founded in the northern metropolises" after the relocation of size-able numbers of African Americans. While it is certainly true that the founders and initial followers of many African American religious sects were graduates of the migratory trail, a closer look reveals a southern origin for a number of black Jewish groups, including the earliest ex-amples of this sectarian genre. This finding suggests the need for a more detailed examination of African American sectarian religious develop-ment in the South prior to World War I. Such an examination would go a long way toward helping us understand why Drake and Cayton, as well as many other observers, encountered such incredible religious diversity as they strolled down the streets of African American neigh-borhoods in northern and midwest metropolises during and after the Great Migration.

African American Mormons in the South

Daryl White and O. Kendall White

For most of its history, the Mormon church has denied access to the temple and priesthood to blacks. Though Brigham Young first announced the priesthood ban in 1849, it evolved out of the slavery controversy. An "invitation" to "free negroes and mulattoes" to join the Mormon community and accusations from established settlers of "tampering with our slaves and endeavoring to sow dissensions and seditions amongst them" (Smith 1978:374–76) ignited the persecution of Mormons in western Missouri. Joseph Smith soon employed the "curse of Canaan" motif of southern Protestantism to legitimate slavery and separate the interests of Mormons from blacks, a tactic that his successors later used to justify denying access to the priesthood and temple to black Latter-day Saints. Few African Americans joined the church during the nineteenth century, and the priesthood taboo became a major source of controversy for the Mormons during the second half of the twentieth century (Bush 1973; Mauss 1981; White 1972, 1981–1982; White and White 1980).

Since lifting the priesthood ban in 1978, the Mormon church has enjoyed phenomenal success among blacks. Though official statistics provide no basis for racial identification, estimates of somewhere between 125,000 and 200,000 blacks throughout the world converted to Mormonism during the decade following their admission to the priesthood (Chandler 1988). While subsequent inactivity is a serious problem, Mormonism apparently has become a means for realizing the American Dream for many African Americans who remain active participants. Indeed, theology, ecclesia, and family reinforce middle-class aspirations and lifestyle. Using data from the Latter-day Saints (LDS) Afro-American Oral History Project, sponsored by the Charles Redd Center at the Brigham Young University, we have examined 110 oral histories of African American Mormons born, raised, or residing in the South to ascertain Mormonism's appeal.[1] We examine the role of theology, participation in the ecclesiastical structure (including integration and segregation), and the significance of family to observe the interplay of race, class, and gender in the southern African American Mormon experience. Before discussing theology, ecclesia, and family, we identify some social background characteristics of African American Mormons who participated in the oral history project.

SOCIAL BACKGROUND CHARACTERISTICS

Data from the oral history project probably tell us less about the class backgrounds of African Americans who join the Mormon church than about those who remain active Latter-day Saints. While aggressively pursuing "active" African American Mormons, the interviewer, Alan Cherry, an African American convert, interviewed only a few "inactive" members. That inactivity is significant may be inferred from the responses of interviewees to Cherry's queries about "other black Latter-day Saints" who no longer participate. It is possible that middle-class African Americans find Mormonism compatible with their experience and aspirations while those from working-class backgrounds find the Mormon community more judgmental and less hospitable and, consequently, leave in disproportionately high numbers.

Be that as it may, Cardell Jacobson's quantitative analysis (1989:14–16) of the entire oral history project, which includes 206 currently available cases, indicates that active African American Mormons are predominantly middle class. Among the 70 percent of the histories in which occupation could be ascertained, two-thirds indicated white collar occupations, including teachers, nurses, journalists, lawyers, musicians, a physician, a pharmacist, a professor emeritus, and a scientist. Sixty-four percent have attended or graduated from college in contrast to 34.6 percent of a national sample of African Americans used for comparison. While only 12 percent of the African American Mormons had less than a high school education, 35 percent of the national sample had not finished high school. If Jacobson (1989:17) has concluded prematurely that African Americans joining the Mormon church are part of Roof and McKinney's "upward" stream of denominational switchers, a socially mobile population typically joining mainline denominations, he certainly appears justified in the assumption that those who remain active demonstrate pronounced middle-class proclivities.

In fact, this assumption enjoys support from the family patterns of these African American Mormons. A majority are married (54.4 percent) or remarried after divorce (9.9 percent), with 18.4 percent remaining single. The spouses of 3.3 percent are deceased, while 17 percent are currently separated or divorced. Approximately 70 percent of those who are married have married only once. Among those with children, the average number is 3.3 (Jacobson 1989:17). A pronounced preoccupation with family and concerns about progress and achievement, as indicated below, characterizes southern African American Mormons.

THEOLOGY

It is hardly accidental that American society—given its preoccupation with work, achievement, and mobility—would sire a religion proclaiming, even more boldly, the American gospel. The optimistic assessment of human potential and the notion of progress so characteristic of American culture became the foundation for the profound this-worldliness of Mormon theology. Fusing religious eschatology with secular reform, Mormonism empowered "ordinary people," to whom power "had been denied in the Jacksonian world of individualism and competition," with clearly defined "beliefs and practices" and a "plan of salvation" that set "Smith and his followers on the road to godhood" (Hansen 1981:82–83).

Nothing was more central to Mormon empowerment than this continuity between the present and future—a denial of the distinction between sacred and secular—embodied in Mormonism's definition of the "next world in terms of this" world. Death became meaningful not as the end of human activity or relations but as a continuation of the same human-divine quest: "eternal progression." God had earned his status, according to the Mormon "law of eternal progression," and human destiny was no less. "As man now is, God once was," proclaimed a popular Mormon saying, and "as God now is, man may become." Thus Mormonism transformed American beliefs in progress and achievement into sacred realities. It projected the fluidity of the class structure, celebrated in national cultural myths, into the beyond. The assertion that a religion that could not save humanity in this life could hardly do so in the next aptly expresses the activist nature of Mormonism.

Not only progress and achievement characterize ultimate reality, but family and church also persist through eternity. Indeed, at a point where the extended, agrarian family was transformed by industrialization, Mormonism affirmed the permanence of kinship with its doctrine of "celestial marriage." So central was the family that an individual could not realize the ultimate destiny of godhood—"exaltation"—outside of marriage. While a celestial marriage, performed in the temple under authority of the priesthood, became a necessary condition for "salvation," other sacraments and ordinances also integrated family and church. In fact, the Mormon preoccupation with genealogy has the ultimate objective of transforming the entire species into a kinship system that corresponds to the ecclesiastical structure. The family is not only a microcosm of the church, but the church is ultimately an extended family (White 1986). Both continue through "time and eternity."

That the Mormon synthesis of the present and future—its integration of life and death, achievement and progress, and family and church— appeals to contemporary African American converts is apparent from their conversion stories. Responses to the interviewer's query about money, for instance, are strikingly middle class. No one identified it as "the root of all evil," as would have been the case with many nineteenth-century converts, and most seemed to integrate economic pursuits with other signs of mastery and achievement. The church's influence might be felt in a new emphasis on frugality and the avoidance of excessive credit manifest in a convert's burning her credit cards ([Cleeretta H. Smiley] *LDS Symposium* 1988), or it may be negligible with others whose attitudes toward money were already consistent with Mormon practice (Albright 1985:22). Noting that she was living the standards of the church before her conversion, Janis Garrison (1985:32–33) describes her future goals in terms of marriage and a "hope to excel in my career and have my own home and just have a happy and wonderful life." For former National Football League rookie of the year, Burgess Owens (*LDS Symposium* 1988), this Mormon pragmatism took priority over any concerns about Mormonism's racial history. "I saw the fruits of the tree," he said, and "if you look at the fruits of the tree and that's what you want for your family, then you pray to the Lord for your answer."

Others found new values, a new lifestyle, and significant changes in self-esteem. Without Mormonism, one convert knew that he would be "dead or in jail." It gave him a "new lifestyle," new aspirations, and "most of all" a "new way to look at myself" (Spencer 1985:6). A "spendaholic" learned to budget, to become a "better wife and mother" while placing many of her aspirations for success in the context of the church. "I hope to be Greensboro's first black Relief Society president," she says, and "I would love to have my husband be a bishop." By being a member, tithing, reading scriptures, remaining active, obeying the "rules and principles," these are "things that you can look forward to. . . . The doors are open now. There is no telling where they could end. There is so much that we could strive for right now. It's like an endless point. That makes me feel good because now I have something I can really look forward to" (Burwell 1989:22).

Though such aspirations are clearly indicative of Mormon conceptions of reality, African American converts often subscribed to these values before joining the church. Mormonism simply imbued middle-class values with ultimate meaning. A coherent theology reinforced extant values and beliefs by rendering them more meaningful. Natheen Albright (1985:5), who converted soon after graduating from New Hampton Institute, succinctly describes this phenomenon: "Everything that they said to me was so logical. It was like I had all the puzzle pieces, but they were just scattered all over the floor. We would have a discussion, and then I would have one whole section of a puzzle put together. It was just like, 'I know that, but how come I don't know that?' It was like I was hearing something that I knew but I did not know I had known."

ECCLESIA

As crucial as this theology may be, the participatory nature of Mormonism appears to be a more compelling reason for African American conversions. Based on a lay ministry, all ecclesiastical offices in the Mormon church, with the exception of the presiding quorums at the apex of the hierarchy, are occupied by unpaid members. Since the church has no professional clergy, a distinction between clergy and laity is meaningless. Indeed, all worthy male Mormons may "hold" the priesthood, conceived as the authority to act in the name of God, and consequently may be "called" to the myriad of offices in the church; these range from bishop—the unpaid, part-time equivalent of a local pastor—and one of his counsellors to a home teacher who visits designated families each month. Though women, who are excluded from the priesthood, enjoy its "blessings" through their husbands or fathers, they too may receive "church callings" to offices not requiring priesthood authority. Since appointments are for limited periods and the church depends on voluntary labor, the number of positions within even a local ward (congregation) is significant. In areas of rapid growth, opportunities abound for active participation.

Consequently, a convert can be involved immediately in religious activity. Though the practice of baptizing, ordaining to the priesthood, and "calling" an inspiring convert to a mission on the same day no longer obtains, African American converts have moved rapidly into ecclesiastical positions at the local level. Upon finding a Mormon pamphlet, Burl Turner, Jr. (1989:5) eagerly informed his wife that "this is about a church that teaches you how to minister." Similarly, Gehrig Harris (1988:14) of White Castle, Louisiana, had prayed "all of these years" for the Lord to utilize his talents when he discovered Mormonism as the "program . . . that could use me."

And use him it did. Following his initial "talk in church," in which he described his conversion and declared that he would "accept to do whatever the Lord would have me do," he has been branch clerk, adviser to the young ladies and their leaders, second counsellor in the branch presidency, first counsellor twice, elders' quorum official, Sunday School teacher, home teacher; his current position is on the stake (diocese) high council. He clearly captures the participatory nature of Mormon ecclesia: "This Church has something for every second, every minute, every hour, every day, every week, every month, every year, that you can involve yourself. There are programs that you can have within your home. You can have programs in others' homes be it visiting or home teaching. In my callings in this Church, I have found that the Lord places me where I can learn. There is no situation that is not a learning situation. He's constantly trying to perfect you, and my testimony is to that" (Harris 1988:15). Harris was baptized in December 1978 and interviewed in June 1987.

Retha Burwell's experience (1989:14) in Greensboro, North Carolina, was no different. "We got baptized one week," she says, and the "following week we were welcomed into the Church. The next week my husband received the Aaronic priesthood, and then the next week the baby was blessed. The following week we both received callings. It was like boom, boom, boom, get them active. But that was fine with us because that is what we wanted to do. After that it was like everything was on a roll and we kept doing more." The fact that all of this activity is voluntary and no one at these levels receives any monetary compensation appealed to many of the African American converts, including Burwell (1989:8–9) who, like many others, is convinced that clergy typically act out of self-interest. She accused her former pastor, a Holiness minister, of owning several airplanes, limos, Rolls Royces, and Cadillacs, in addition to seducing women and molesting children. Though not so graphic or harsh in their accusations, other African American converts shared her anticlerical sentiments.

In addition to the "callings" and offices, the participatory nature of religious services themselves—the language, dress, and individual use of the priesthood—reinforce a particularly appealing sense of egalitarianism. Some converts found this in the testimony meeting, a monthly service in which people speak of the value of the church in their lives, and in other Sacrament Meetings such as Sunday worship services, when speakers are selected from the congregation in contrast to the sermons of a professional clergy. The ordinary attire of Mormons and lack of clerical robes, which differentiate clergy from laity in Protestant and Catholic congregations, enhanced this sense of equality. When the non-Mormon extended family of Betty Baunchand (1988:6) attended her grandmother's funeral and discovered their kinfolk speaking, offering the prayers, singing the songs, and playing the piano, they were astounded, having "never seen anything like that before." In their churches, the "minister or the deacons prepare the service and families just sit in the audience."

As appealing as the participatory nature of Mormon eccelesia may be, the question of integration remains unanswered. How have southern African American Mormons fared? Since the oral histories are primarily limited to active Latter-day Saints, they clearly underreport problems of prejudice and discrimination. Even so, race relations are often identified as the primary cause for inactivity among other African Americans and as a problem for many of the interviewees. As elsewhere in American society, racial conflict exacerbates tendencies toward segregation and separation.

The church has a history of voluntary separation manifest in special purpose associations and congregations, typically based on ethnicity, age, or marital status. Occasionally immigrants organized special wards with services in their native languages, but these were temporary means of socialization into Mormonism rather than vehicles for preserving immigrant culture. Though many participants in the oral history project speak of a desire to preserve basic elements of their African American heritage, the special black organizations seem to follow the typical pattern for earlier immigrant groups. Genesis groups, the original form organized in Salt Lake City in the early seventies, have appeared among African American Mormons as a means of mutual contact and to address unique problems. As meaningful as they may be to individuals, they have had a short life span. Claiming that the Washington, D.C., Genesis group was one of her most significant experiences in the church, Cleeretta Smiley (*LDS Symposium* 1988) linked its demise to internal problems, even though it had assisted the church with public relations problems for the Caribbean islands and Cleveland, Ohio, contributed to missionary efforts, and was in the process of recovering black Mormon history.

In at least one case, segregation provided the impetus for separate congregations. The missionaries' preoccupation with the rapid conversion of African Americans conflicted with the interests of an established white congregation in Charlotte, North Carolina. Ostensibly providing opportunities for inner city blacks who lacked transportation to the suburban chapel and easing "tension whites and blacks felt" worshipping together, mission President Ralph Bradley established an African American branch (Embry 1990:2). Missionaries had described Mormon welfare programs while proselytizing in public housing projects and circumvented a rule requiring converts to attend one Sacrament Meeting prior to baptism by hastily arranging meetings minutes before performing the ceremony. Substantial numbers joined the church, but a significant majority soon fell away. Membership figures of nine to twelve hundred were given to independent observers in 1986 and 1988, though church attendance dropped below two hundred (Embry 1990:21). Perhaps class differences between these converts and more typical middle-class African American Mormons account for the former's inactivity as well as the missionaries' subsequent lack of concern.

A special African American congregation also appeared in Greensboro, North Carolina. Initiated by black Mormons, it too was a result of prejudice. Following Johnnie McKoy's calling as ward mission leader, African American membership grew to four hundred. But many of the new converts soon became inactive, convinced they were not welcome in the church. With the creation of a special branch, seventy-five inactive converts immediately returned to church (*LDS Symposium* 1988). In June 1988 this branch was virtually 90 percent black, averaged four baptisms a month, and had a 60-percent retention rate, with approximately 150 active members (Embry 1990:22).

Not surprisingly, black Latter-day Saints react ambivalently to these "special" congregations. To many, the separate branch or ward is an anathema. Retha Burwell (1989:13), for example, did not appreciate missionaries taking her family to Greensboro's Second Ward "because it had more blacks." "I am not comfortable in that ward," she said, "I like to be in a mixed congregation." She describes her experience after "getting the missionaries to take us to our correct ward": "The first Sunday there we had four dinner invitations. We had people that wanted to come over and visit, and people were telling us how happy they were that we joined, how much they loved us. None of these were blacks [*sic*] people because we did not have that many black people in our ward at that time. All of these members were white. I love every last one of them."

Yet, the Burwells have not escaped prejudice. Having dinner at a white Latter-day Saint's home, they were told that the special branch was being formed because "white folks cannot handle the fact that we have blacks in the ward." She replied, "Who cares if the white people like us being in the Church or not. You were the ones that came and knocked on my door. I did not go to you." She responded in a similar manner to a prejudiced missionary. " 'You need to go home because the majority of the people you are going to be teaching in the area where you are at is us. If you cannot handle us, you need to tell them to put you in an all white area then because we are not going to stop joining the Church. We have got our chance now; we are coming in there. We are going to get in there, and we are not going to leave.' Now he and I have a really good friendship" (Burwell 1989:12).

There is evidence of more successful integration. Told that some whites might leave the church because of African American conversions, Van C. Wright, Sr. (1989:18), from Baker, Louisiana, observed that this was "just a weeding out process." He had experienced some slights and avoidance from a bishop whose ward he was visiting as a member of the stake high council, but he is convinced that "people are learning down South" and that "in Baker they can't do without us. We're part of the family now." He has never felt really unwanted. "From day one, I didn't feel like I was a stranger. Now they might have felt that. They may have felt like their home was being invaded or something, but when I went to church that first day, I felt like I was where I was supposed to be. I felt like that was the Church I had been going to all my life. When I first went, it was just like I had been there. I'm not bothered by it at all."

The experience of Clement Biggs (1989:7–8), from Birmingham, Alabama, illustrates the educational value of integration for white Mormons. When the elder's quorum had planned bowling activities for their families, they discovered that a Christian fellowship league controlled the alley on Friday nights. Thinking that this would protect them from the typical atmosphere and "foul language," they requested and received an invitation to participate in the league. Because of his work schedule, the Biggs family did not attend the first evening. However, the following Friday, as the group put on their bowling shoes, the non-Mormons huddled in a corner. A representative of the latter soon approached, explaining that the Christian Fellowship League was for white people. It was his young daughter's first "real encounter with prejudice," and Biggs took her from the bowling alley while requesting that their friends please "go on and bowl." He had no desire to "cause any trouble" nor to "interfere with their fun." To his surprise, "Everybody from our branch came on out. They weren't going to bowl. If we couldn't bowl, they weren't going to bowl. We got outside and we talked about it then. The man there gave us our money back. The Church was behind us. They came out with us, and they stopped bowling with these people. They stopped even going to that bowling alley. They even talked about calling in some reporters and telling them what happened. I didn't want them to go that far. We all stood outside. We hugged, and we had tears. We got in our cars and went our own ways."

Biggs's experience within the church reflects Mormon egalitarianism. The use of kinship categories of "brother" and "sister," in both religious and social contexts, suggests social equality for him. For older southern African Americans, whose experience with forms of address as a mechanism of social control is legendary, such language may be

particularly important. Having been denied the common courtesy of
"Mr." and "Mrs.," presumably entitled by age and marital status alone,
the application of "brother" and "sister" to black and white alike was
inclusive and egalitarian. It was simply too good to be true, for Biggs
(1989:8–9), so it must be "fake." "I was born in this town," he says,
"these people can't really mean this." So he decided to talk with children whom he believed would have greater difficulty disguising their
attitudes. He stopped them in the hall, shook their hands, and introduced himself. He continues: "These children talked and acted the same
as their parents acted. They would ask me, 'Are you a member of our
Church?' I would say, 'Yes, I was baptized the other day.' They would
say, 'You are our brother then aren't you?' I said, 'You mean that everybody that is baptized into the Church is your brother?' They said, 'If
you're a Latter-day Saint, you're our brother.' Some of them called me
Mr. Biggs, and when I told them that I was baptized, then they said,
'You're supposed to be called Brother Biggs.' " Convinced that the
"children are being taught this," he observes that these are the people
who "have really helped hold me in the Church." They "are really trying to overcome," teaching their children "right principles," "not to
hate this man because he is brown or black. . . . If he is a member of the
Church, he is your brother, no matter who he is" (Biggs 1989:9).

FAMILY

The kinship categories of brother and sister not only suggest egalitarianism, but they integrate church and family. The unique religious
significance of the family, as we have already observed, is grounded in
its metaphysical status as an "eternal" institution, a position shared with
only one other institution—the church. In the Mormon experience, the
ideal family is, in a profound sense, a microcosm of the church. As
head of the family, the father may bless, baptize, ordain, and "anoint
and administer" (a healing ritual) to his wife and children. That many
converts found "exercising their priesthood" meaningful is evident in
the frequency of blessing children at the beginning of the school year,
when faced with other challenges, or simply upon feeling the need;
the pleasure expressed in the baptizing and confirming of family and
friends; and the gratification from "anointing and administering to the

sick" in the home, community, or hospital. Such use of the priesthood occasionally produced a sense of psychological healing and improved race relations, as, for instance, when Van Wright, Sr. (1989:18) and his brother-in-law blessed a "white brother" whose racism had been obvious at the time Wright joined the church.

The family structure thus becomes a reflection of ecclesiastical structure, with the father presiding over his family as Christ presides over the church. Excluded from the priesthood, women remain dependent upon men for the blessings and sacraments noted above. With the sacralization of the roles of women in reproduction, nurturing of children, and support of the family, patriarchal kinship and ecclesiastical structures, which preserve female subordination, are legitimated. Though women cannot be saved (exalted) without men, neither can men be exalted without women. Only through the bonds of a celestial marriage can men and women realize their ultimate destinies.

While buttressing Mormon opposition to feminism and the Equal Rights Amendment (White 1989), these social structures and theology enjoy enthusiastic support from African American Mormons. The patriarchal family is viewed by many women as requiring men to assume their obligations to provide for and sustain the family. Burgess Owens was praised by black LDS women at a Brigham Young University symposium for assuming an appropriate role as head of his family (*LDS Symposium* 1988) and Janis Garrison (1985:13–15), who grew up in Arkansas, documents prevailing attitudes by her own dissent in her discussion of dating at Brigham Young University. Characterizing herself as no "Betty BYU," she laments male students' preoccupation with finding a "homemaker." Surely there must be some men who want "balance"—"more of a career oriented person"—but she has not found them. "Guys in this community, where they are the patriarch, feel they have to be domineering, they have to wear the pants in the family and 'I am not going to have no woman tell me what to do.' I go against this norm all the way. I guess when it comes down to deciding on a wife, the guy would say, 'Do I want her as a wife?' I guess it is easier for a guy to go out and find some girl who will henpeck him and who can make bread for him and pop out babies every nine months. If that is what they want, then fine. They are not worth my time and energy." Perceiving her position as marginal, she correctly identifies typical sentiments of participants in the oral history project.

It is also evident that African American converts see the family as a microcosm of the church in another sense, that is, as the principal training ground for success in the church and community. More devoted commitment to the official objectives of family home evening, a church program for weekly family activities, is difficult to imagine. In fact, the typical family home evening is a ritual reproduction of the Mormon worship service with opening and closing prayers, punctuated by songs, scripture readings, talks by the children, and a lesson. Children may be encouraged to pray, as in Burl Turner's family (1989:12), for "the things they need in life like going to school" and "making good grades in their exams." Elizabeth Pulley (1985:8), with her husband and five children, provides a textbook example of family home evening in the following description:

> When we have family home evening, one will give the scripture, one will give the closing prayer, and one will give the opening prayer. Each one of them will get to sing their favorite song. Then Andrew or I will do the lesson. Some nights instead of having a lesson we have game nights where we just play games. Other times we have what we call discussions where we discuss family rules, rules of going to school and what they should learn and how they should obey. Then we have times during family home evening where we discuss how they are progressing in their classes, what they are learning, and how much they are learning.

Family home evening is occasionally used as a pretext for encouraging others. When Turner (1989:12) discovered that people under his "stewardship" were not holding family home evening, he incorporated them into his family home evenings until they started their own. Addressing problems of single parents, Natheen Albright (1985:8) characterized her organization in California, which integrated several single-parent families into a shared family home evening, as comparable to those she had experienced in Arlington, Virginia. While some use family home evening to enhance social cohesion in their extended families, others encourage active participation by non-Mormon kinfolk on a routine basis. Occasionally a "family home evening" becomes a pretext for creating artificial families (fictive kinship) on college campuses in order to involve single students in a "family atmosphere."

Thus, the family in Mormonism enjoys a metaphysical status comparable only to ecclesia; it is a unit of the church—the church in miniature—with the priesthood vested in the patriarchal father. With Mormon ecclesia and worship ritually reproduced in the family home evening, the family becomes the principal socialization agent for church and society at the same time kinship categories enable a literalistic conceptualization of the church as extended family. Apparently this unique integration of individual, family, and church is especially appealing to contemporary middle-class African American converts to Mormonism.

CONCLUSION

If its response to slavery left Mormonism with a racist legacy ensuring little African American participation until revocation of the priesthood ban in 1978, today thousands of African Americans find Mormon theology, ecclesia, and family meaningful. Providing a coherent theological foundation for American values and beliefs in progress and achievement, Mormonism sacralized an activist middle-class lifestyle, denying excessive individualism by embedding it within the structures of ecclesia and kinship.

Opportunities for active participation in ecclesiastical offices and rapid upward mobility in the church are obviously appealing factors in the conversion and continuing participation of middle-class African American Mormons in the South. Though prejudice and discrimination still reinforce processes of segregation and separation and undoubtedly contribute to disproportionately high levels of inactivity among black Latter-day Saints, the emergent tendencies toward integration auger well for the continuation and expansion of Mormonism among southern African Americans. The appointment in April of a black Brazilian elder to one of the highest ecclesiastical offices may encourage even greater mobility for southern African American Latter-day Saints in their movement from the branch and ward (parish) to stake (diocese) levels. In fact, it was the participatory quality of Mormon ecclesia that southern African American converts identified as the most compelling basis of egalitarianism.

If race is becoming less of an obstacle to equality, gender remains firmly ensconced in the patriarchal family and church. The "eternal family" assumes a male head with the priesthood as the link between kinship and ecclesia. Rarely did the oral histories indicate dissatisfaction with the patriarchal family for either women or men. Indeed, the fact that the eternal family assumes a father and mother—that neither men nor women can be exalted outside the bonds of marriage—was very appealing to both male and female converts in the South. Moreover, this linkage between kinship and ecclesia has become the structural basis for the organization of their lives, and if Mormon integration is successful, it is likely to enhance the appeal of Mormonism to southern African Americans in the immediate future.

NOTE

1. We wish to thank the Charles Redd Center and the Brigham Young University Archives for providing access to the oral histories, and especially Professor Jessie Embry who, in addition to her generous assistance, also made helpful comments on this paper. Financial support for our research was provided by Bush Faculty Development grants from Spelman College and Glenn grants from Washington and Lee University during the summers of 1988 and 1989.

Epilogue

Brett Williams

In keeping with a turn in our discipline, this collection of papers by anthropologists is actually a collection of histories. Some eye southern culture at the turn of the century, when African Americans experienced mass disenfranchisement and segregation, forced labor through debt and convict peonage, sadistic lynchings, lashings, and torture. They survey the space blacks struggled to build within Jim Crow: through shared food and healing traditions, mutual aid societies, and the black nationalist and Holiness churches. They help us understand how that oppressive period left its ugly mark and why the response to it sometimes seems so strained and strange.

These papers also help us see culture more clearly *as* history, although there is fruitful disagreement about how culture works. Some see it as adaptive, tenacious, meaningful, and worthy of respect on its own terms. Others see cracks and contradictions. Some struggle for new ways of conceptualizing cultural processes, but most point to the importance of seeing culture in history, and southern culture as part of a larger history. The South is not simply a periphery, and southerners are not marginal after all.

This collection also raises major questions about the political mystique of the African American church. Merrill Singer and Hans Baer argue that black Judaism and Pentecostalism rose out of hard times to comment on oppression and shelter the oppressed, yet became regressive, hegemonic institutions themselves. Daryl and Kendall White describe middle-class Mormons embracing tired visions of progress and upward mobility. These diverse churches remind us that the black church is not a homogeneous place. But interesting questions rise as well from Ira Harrison's work in Happy Valley, Tennessee. He seems, reasonably enough, to have sought out local ministers as natural community leaders in AIDS prevention. While frustrated in his efforts to work with them, he concludes his essay with a plea that they exercise political leadership.

Political scientist Adolph Reed (1986) argues that many Americans wrongly see the church as the ultimate source of *political* legitimacy for African Americans, evidenced, for example, by Jesse Jackson's crusade for electoral ordination there. The church played many political and social roles during a time when blacks were denied access to other institutions. But Reed believes that throughout much of this century, mainline black churches have been quiescent and conservative, that even their role during the civil rights movement has been overblown. Dr. Martin Luther King, Jr., railed against the resistance of church leaders to the Montgomery bus boycott, and much of the initiative in other campaigns came from groups such as student organizations. Reed argues that many churches' main contribution was to lend their facilities for meetings organized by other groups.

Perhaps Reed's claims are too strong, but I was fascinated that Harrison's experiences in Happy Valley so closely bore them out. Hilda and Charles Williams also see the mutual aid societies inspired by churches as politically ambiguous, functioning more for social control than social change. When has religion been a force for social change, when not, and why? Have we miscast ministers as protest leaders? Where were they in Bordertown, when the elite built a split labor market that pushed would-be entrepreneurs into plantation-style work? Do the churches that seem so meaningful to residents of North Carolina and Georgia also fight for better health care? When do ministers march to the tune of their congregations, as Harrison claims? When and how do members of their congregations mobilize other networks to push them forward?

This leads me to my major concern with this collection, which looks at gender just enough to make me want to know much more. The authors hint at sexism as a social force that abets racism. We learn that the dominant culture has devalued both midwifery and food, domains of autonomy and control for African American women. We see women's skills used against them when they became threatening. Even oppositional churches offer women few blessings. The Mormons promise racial equality, but women and men can seek salvation only in husband-dominated nuclear family households, although many African Americans may participate in more extended, flexible, female-centered domestic networks.

Beyond these blatant ways to divide women and men, they may experience the same social problem in different ways. For example, employers and elites use gender and race in creative and distracting ways to recruit and exploit labor. Singer argues that new opportunities to work on the railroads and in merchant ships broadened the horizons of African Americans and opened them up to Judaism. By African Americans Singer most likely means men. Did women's work change as well? Whose changing employment influenced the adoption of a liberating theology within a patriarchal frame, and how?

Carole Hill's hard-hitting examination of disease and mortality also collapses the experiences of women and men in several ways. On all national measures the gap between white and black men has increased, but for women the picture is much more complex. Yet Hill seems to conclude by allowing the gap for men to stand for everybody. In looking at Coberly, she ignores any differences altogether. She might make an even more powerful argument by taking gender differences seriously and asking why they occur. *Who* had problems with heart and blood, diabetes, arthritis, and rheumatism? Why the enormous increase in influenza and pneumonia among black women in the 1980s? If black women (but not men) appear to be doing better against heart disease, stroke, and cancer, why are maternal and infant mortality such persistent problems, why so many hysterectomies, and why does Hill conclude that the *real* problems are drug abuse, alcoholism, and AIDS? A "community" or institution may be a single homogeneous structure, but then again it may not, and it can't hurt to check. Women and men may experience and perceive community life differently, and part of thinking about African Americans as diverse citizens means looking at those differences.

Another way to take gender seriously is to pay full attention to female agency. This does not mean assuming that all women are the same or that all women are morally superior to all men, but simply looking at what women do (Leonardo 1991). Some of the authors do this, while some do not. Most did not know that what they were describing might emerge elsewhere. I was struck, for example, by how often women's personal networks emerged as important: in carving out a precious, autonomous space for controlling childbirth and pre- and postnatal care in eastern North Carolina, drawing on kin and friends to build an entire congregation for the Church of God in Christ, and organizing against AIDS in Happy Valley, Tennessee. Perhaps our preoccupation with the role of male ministers has prevented us from paying full attention to these networks. Karen Sacks (1988) has documented their crucial role in the Duke University Hospital union drives of the 1970s; they might also underlie the apparently successful strike of African American women in Indianola, Mississippi, against Delta Catfish, Inc.

Why do women do what they do and how do they perceive it? How do North Carolina women of different generations and domestic situations evaluate their work at preparing food and gathering and keeping kin? What are the economic consequences of these activities? Do women and men share ideas about health and illness, about the body and how it should work, about symptoms that are inevitable, and about when to seek care? Do some act as caretakers for others' health? Who do people discuss health behavior with, and why? What are the women's auxiliaries of the Church of God in Christ, what do they do, and why does COGIC also have a "Women's Department"?

There is nothing natural or inevitable about the shape black Judaism or black Holiness churches took, especially at the turn of the century. (As one of many examples of varied utopian/spiritual communities, the Texas Sanctifications were a group of somewhat racist white women who swore celibacy and economic independence from men.) The whites take women's voices seriously, and doing so helps enormously to elucidate the appeal as well as the frustrations of black Mormonism. Could other black church women help illuminate what drew them to these religions, how they saw their place in a patriarchal congregation, how they worked to recruit kin and friends for networks, and when they mobilized those networks for political ends, as David's sister Fannie did in Happy Valley?

African American mutual aid societies have certainly been powerful self-help organizations, as Hilda and Charles Williams claim. I would love to know more about them, and here again I think gender helps provide a thicker picture. Which were organized by women, which by men? Were some inclusive and some not? When and why? Some were obviously fraternal, but how were those different from the Sons and Daughters of Esther or the Brothers and Sisters of Love? The Williams summarize the goals of mutual aid societies as charity, education, socialization, and social control. But we could learn much from untangling those goals and learning who did what, when, and why. For example, Mississippi probably experienced the fiercest Jim Crow regime of any state; African Americans had no vote and almost no leverage under what was essentially a reign of terror. Yet by adopting a social housekeeping posture, the Mississippi Federation of Colored Women's Clubs fought for the education of handicapped children and "training schools" for juvenile delinquents. It convinced the state government to add a black wing to its tuberculosis hospital (McMillen 1989). How did women's experiences compare with men's at the black colleges that rose out of these societies? How did they create and experience those school's injunctions to purchase real estate, avoid intemperance, or cultivate true manhood?

We also need to think about how different social actors use gender to talk and think about what's going on. Southern African Americans negotiate a wide world of meanings and symbols in this volume. These include many that people surely build themselves, on the ground, about kin and community, sugar and salt, corn and pork, and how to live in one's body. Many others are imposed or imported from larger traditions: Egyptian servitude, resistance and Exodus, the American Dream, the plantation past.

Do people talk about health and illness without talking about different male and female bodies? Why "the curse of Eve" to frame childbirth, in a situation controlled by local women? How do kin terms reinvent certain kinds of families and households as divinely ordained? Why a "Mother Church" for COGIC or "celestial marriage" for the Mormons? Why the seemingly egalitarian language, "Brothers and Sisters," to talk about mutual aid or religious community? Southern African Americans drew on the potentially liberating language of the Hebrew Bible to frame black Judaism and also to name mutual aid societies. Most of the great prophets and patriarchs were, of course, men, thus Tubman and Truth, real-life models, get likened to Moses or Joshua. Why does Esther (rather than, say, Judith) emerge as this volume's sole Hebrew heroine? Esther cultivated her beauty and passed as a non-Jew to replace a disobedient wife in the harem of a Persian king. Her test of courage involved preparing a sumptuous dinner for the king in order to persuade him not to kill the Jews; eventually he even allowed them to organize to defend themselves. How did women and men perceive Esther as a symbol during the Jim Crow era? How do they talk about her today?

The dominant theme in discussing African Americans today is sociologist William J. Wilson's conception of a pathological underclass, created by racist institutions but to be recognized by dysfunctional behaviors, particularly of its women (Wilson 1987; see also Reed 1988). Happily, these authors by and large rebut that notion, for it has cut a wide swath across journalistic popular culture. Yet it is a pesky, pernicious concept that fights to get in.

Yet while this book banishes the nasty underclass, the African Americans who remain seem awfully accommodative. This may just reflect the luck of the draw. This portrait may also reflect these studies' roots in Jim Crow, when resistance was very dangerous. Yet, although resistance was hard, messianic nationalism was but one type of strategy during that era. In 1889, for example, black Mississippians gathered to suppress the cruel suppression of the black vote, and the Colored Farmers Alliance organized to gain greater bargaining power for tenants. In 1904 black citizens in five Mississippi cities boycotted the newly segregated streetcars. African Americans sometimes protested the use of their taxes to build white schools, and often raised money to build their own. The same society that witnessed the emergence of the black Holiness churches also saw the fiery Ida B. Wells rail against lynching in Memphis *Free Speech*. The civil rights movement grew slowly from this range of ways blacks found to cope with and protest injustice. I wonder if more digging might uncover some of this range: among the granny midwives or in the rural southern communities studied by Whitehead and Hill. Culture may, in the long run, be something like an argument, and while anthropologists can be astute social critics, others engage in the debate as well.

References

Abrahams, Roger, 1984. Equal Opportunity Eating: A Structural Excursus on Things of the Mouth. In *Ethnic and Regional Foodways in the United States: The Performance of Group Identity*, L. F. Brown and K. Mussel, eds. (Knoxville: University of Tennessee Press), pp. 19–36.

Ahlstorm, Sydney E., 1975. *A Religious History of the American People*, vol. 2 (Garden City, N.Y.: Image Books).

Albright, Natheen, 1985. Oral history, interviewed by Alan Cherry, 23 Oct., LDS Afro-American, Brigham Young University.

Alexis, Marcus, 1974. The Political Economy of Labor Market Discrimination: Synthesis and Exploration. In *Patterns of Discrimination*, vol. 2, A. Von Furstenberg, ed. (Lexington, Mass.: D. C. Heath), pp. 63–83.

Alkalimat, Abdul, 1986. *Introduction to Afro-American Studies: A Peoples Primer* (Chicago: Twenty-first Century).

Almer, Robert W., and H. Bruce Dull, eds., 1987. *Closing the Gap: The Burden of Unnecessary Illness* (New York: Oxford University Press).

Anderson, Robert Mapes, 1979. *Vision of the Disinherited: The Making of American Pentecostalism* (New York: Oxford University Press).

Aptheker, Herbert, 1939. Maroons Within the Present Limits of the United States. *Journal of Negro History* 24:167–84.

Ardener, Shirley, 1964. The Comparative Study of Rotating Credit Associations. *Journal of Royal Anthropological Institute* 99:201–29.

Austin, Diane J., 1981. Born Again . . . And Again and Again: Communitas and Social Change Among Jamaican Pentecostalists. *Journal of Anthropological Research* 37:226–46.

Baer, Hans A., 1982. Toward a Systematic Typology of Black Folk Healers. *Phylon* 43:327–43.

——— , 1984. *The Black Spiritual Movement* (Knoxville: University of Tennessee Press).

——— , 1985. Spiritual Israelites in a Small Southern City: Elements of Protest and Accommodation in Belief and Oratory. *Southern Quarterly* 23:103–24.

——— , 1988. Black Mainstream Churches: Emancipatory or Accommodative Responses to Racism and Social Stratification in American Society? *Review of Religious Research* 30:162–76.

Baer, Hans, and Merrill Singer, 1981. Toward a Typology of Black Sectarian-

References

ism as a Response to Racial Stratification. *Anthropological Quarterly* 54:1–14.

Barnes, Annie S., 1986. *Black Women: Interpersonal Relationships in Profile* (Bristol, Ind.: Wyndham Hall Press).

——— , 1987. *Single Parents in Black America* (Bristol, Ind.: Wyndham Hall Press).

——— , 1989. Single Mothers in Black Colleges. In *Women in the South,* Holly F. Mathews, ed. (Athens: University of Georgia Press), pp. 47–56.

——— , 1990. Black Single Fathers: Continuity, Neutrality, and Change. *Virginia Social Science Journal* 25:93–101.

Battie, Allen Overton, 1961. Status Personality in a Negro Holiness Sect (Ph.D. diss., Catholic University of America).

Baunchand, Betty W., 1988. Oral history, interviewed by Alan Cherry, 10 June 1987, LDS Afro-American, Brigham Young University.

Beardsley, Edward H., 1987. *A History of Neglect: Health Care for Blacks and Millworkers in the Twentieth-Century South* (Knoxville: University of Tennessee).

Becker, Gary, 1957. *The Economics of Discrimination* (Chicago: University of Chicago Press).

Bender, Thomas, 1975. *Toward an Urban Vision: Ideas and Institutions in Nineteenth Century America* (Lexington: University of Kentucky Press).

Bennett, John W., 1943. Food and Social Status in a Rural Society. *American Sociological Review* 8:561–69.

Berger, Graenum, 1978. *Black Jews in America* (New York: Commission on Synagogue Relations).

Berkeley, Kathleen C., 1980. Like a Plague of Locusts: Immigration and Social Change in Memphis, Tennessee, 1850–1880 (unpublished manuscript).

Berliner, Howard S., 1985. *A System of Scientific Medicine: Philanthropic Foundations in the Flexner Era* (London and New York: Tavistock).

Bernard, Jessie, 1966. *Marriage and Family Among Negroes* (Englewood Cliffs, N.J.: Prentice-Hall).

Berreman, Gerald D., 1962. *Behind Many Masks: Ethnography and Impression Management in a Himalayan Village* [1930]. Ithaca, N.Y.: Society for Applied Anthropology.

Biggs, Clement C., 1989. Oral history, interviewed by Alan Cherry, 3 June 1987, LDS Afro-American, Brigham Young University.

Blanks, Delilah, 1984. Cultural Continuity and Change in Food Habits in Southern Black Families. (Ph.D. diss., University of North Carolina, Chapel Hill).

Bleich, J. David, 1972. Black Jews: A Halakhic Perspective. *Tradition: A Journal of Orthodox Jewish Thought* 15:48–79.

Blisset, Diane, 1987. Factors Relating to High Infant Mortality Rates in a Rural Georgia County (unpublished paper).

Bloch, Judy, 1990. Edgecombe Is Battling to Save Its Babies. *News and Observer* (Raleigh, N.C.), 1 Apr., pp. A1, A12.

Boggs, Beverly, 1977. Some Aspects of Worship in a Holiness Church. *New York Folklore* 3:29–44.

Bonacich, Edna, 1976. Advanced Capitalism and Black/White Race Relations in the United States: A Split Labor Market Interpretation. *American Sociological Review* 41:34–51.

Breeden, James O., 1988. Disease as a Factor in Southern Distinctiveness. In *Disease and Distinctiveness in the American South*, Todd L. Savitt and James Harvey Young, eds. (Knoxville: University of Tennessee Press).

Brewer, J. S., 1928. The Responsibility of the Public in the Matter of Maternal and Infant Mortality. *North Carolina State Board of Health Bulletin* 43(6): 5–8.

Brotz, Howard, 1952. Negro "Jews" in the United States. *Phylon* 13:324–37.

———, 1970. *The Black Jews of Harlem* (New York: Schocken Books).

Brown, Diane Robinson, 1982. *The Church as a Predictor of Black Social Participation in Voluntary Associations* (Washington, D.C.: Mental Health Research and Development Center and the Institute for Urban Affairs and Research, Howard University).

Bullard, Robert D., ed., 1989. *In Search of the New South: The Black Urban Experience in the 1970s and 1980s* (Tuscaloosa: University of Alabama Press).

Bullard, Robert D., and Beverley Hendrix Wright, 1986. The Politics of Pollution: Implications for the Black Community. *Phylon* 47:71–78.

Bureau of the Census, 1986. *Household After-Tax Income: 1986*. Current Population Reports, Special Studies, series P. 12, no. 157 (Washington, D.C.: Government Printing Office).

———, 1989. *Money Income and Poverty Status in the United States: 1988*. Current Population Reports: Consumer Income. Bureau of the Census, series P. 60, no. 166 (Washington, D.C.: Government Printing Office).

Burns, Thomas A., and J. Stephen Smith, 1978. The Symbolism of Becoming in the Sunday Service of an Urban Black Holiness Church. *Anthropological Quarterly* 51:184–204.

Burwell, Retha, 1989. Oral history, interviewed by Alan Cherry, 25 Jan. 1986, LDS Afro-American, Brigham Young University.

Bush, Lester E., 1973. Mormonism's Negro Doctrine: An Historical Overview. *Dialogue* 23(1):11–37.

Cartwright, Fredrick Fox, 1972. *Disease and History* (New York: Crowell).

Center for Health Services Research and Development, 1988. *Statistics on Physician Availability in Eastern North Carolina* (Greenville, N.C.: East Carolina University School of Medicine).

——, 1989. *Educational Training Program for Community Health Advocacy* (Greenville, N.C.: East Carolina University School of Medicine).

Chandler, Russell, 1988. Mormonism: A Challenge for Blacks. *Los Angeles Times*, 12 Aug.

Church of God in Christ, 1973. *Official Manual with the Doctrines and Discipline of the Church of God in Christ* (Memphis, Tenn.: Church of God in Christ).

——, 1985. *Minutes of the General Assembly, April 13–15, 1985* (Memphis, Tenn.: Church of God in Christ).

Clark, William A., 1937. Sanctification in Negro Religion. *Social Forces* 15:544–51.

Cooper, George M., 1937. Progress in Maternal and Child Health Work. *North Carolina State Board of Health Bulletin* 52(1):5–9.

Courlander, Harold, 1966. *Negro Folk Music, U.S.A.* (London: Jazz Book Club).

Cussler, Margaret, and M. L. deGive, 1953. *'Twixt the Cup and Lip': Psychological and Sociocultural Factors Affecting Food Habits* (New York: Twayne).

Davis, Allison, Burleigh B. Gardner, and Mary R. Gardner, 1941. *Deep South: A Social Anthropological Study of Caste and Class* (Chicago: University of Chicago Press).

Davis, Angela Y., 1981. *Women, Race, & Class* (New York: Vintage Books).

Davis, Linwood G., 1980. The Politics of Black Self-Help in the United States: A Historical Overview. In *Black Organizations: Issues on Survival Techniques*, Lennox S. Yearwood, ed. (Washington, D.C.: University Press of America), pp. 37–50.

de Garine, Igor, 1971. The Sociocultural Aspects of Nutrition. *Ecology of Food and Nutrition* 1:143–63.

De Lee, Joseph B., 1915. Progress Toward Ideal Obstetrics. *Transactions of the American Association for the Study and Prevention of Infant Mortality* 6:114–23.

Dellinger, Anne, 1983. North Carolina Health Legislation in 1983. *Health Law Bulletin* 64:1–6.

Devitt, Neal, 1979a. The Statistical Case for Elimination of the Midwife: Fact Versus Prejudice, 1890–1935 (Part 1). *Women and Health* 4(1):81–96.

——, 1979b. The Statistical Case for Elimination of the Midwife: Fact Versus Prejudice, 1890–1935 (Part 2). *Women and Health* 4(2):169–85.

Dollard, John, 1937. *Caste and Class in a Southern Town* (New Haven, Conn.: Yale University Press).

Dougherty, Molly C., 1978a. Southern Lay Midwives as Ritual Specialists. In *Women in Ritual and Symbolic Roles*, J. Hoch-Smith and Anita Spring, eds. (New York: Plenum Press), pp. 151–64.

————, 1978b. *Becoming a Woman in Rural Black Culture* (New York: Holt, Rinehart and Winston).

————, 1982. Southern Midwifery and Organized Health Care: Systems in Conflict. *Medical Anthropology* 6:114–26.

Drake, St. Clair, 1965. The Social and Economic Status of the Negro in the United States. *Journal of the American Academy of Arts and Sciences* 94: 771–814.

Drake, St. Clair, and Horace R. Cayton, 1945. *Black Metropolis* (New York: Harper).

————, 1962. *Black Metropolis*, vol. 2 (New York: Harper and Row).

DuBois, W. E. B., 1899. *The Philadelphia Negro* (Philadelphia: University of Pennsylvania).

————, 1907. *Economic Cooperation Among American Negroes* (Atlanta: Atlanta University Press).

Eddy, G. Norman, 1952. Store-Front Religion. In *Cities and Churches: Readings on the Urban Church*, Robert Lee, ed. (Philadelphia: Westminster), pp. 177–94.

Edgerton, John, 1987. *Southern Food: At Home, on the Road, in History* (New York: Alfred A. Knopf).

Elkins, Stanley M., 1959. *Slavery: A Problem in American Institutional and Intellectual Life* (Chicago: University of Chicago Press).

Ellis, Bernard A., 1990. The HIV/AIDS Epidemic Among Blacks in Tennessee: A Review of AIDS Surveillance and HIV Seroprevalence Data. AIDS Surveillance and Seroprevalence, Tennessee AIDS Program.

Ellwood, David, 1988. *Poor Support* (New York: Basic Books).

Embry, Jessie L., 1990. "Separate but Equal?" Black Branches, Genesis Groups, or Integrated Wards. *Dialogue* 23(1):11–37.

Evans, Cherie, 1990. Making an Investment in Life. *Daily Reflector* (Greenville, N.C.), 12 Aug., Sec. C, p. 1.

Fauset, Arthur Huff, 1971. *Black Gods of the Metropolis* (Philadelphia: University of Pennsylvania Press).

Feagin, Joe R., and Clairece Booher Feagin, 1978. *Discrimination American Style: Institutional Racism and Sexism* (Englewood Cliffs, N.J.: Prentice-Hall).

Fitzgerald, Thomas, 1979. "Southern Folks' Eating Habits Ain't What They Used To Be . . . If They Ever Were." *Nutrition Today*, July/August, pp. 16–21.

Ford, Thomas R., 1978. Contemporary Rural America: Persistence and Change. In *Rural USA: Persistence and Change*, T. R. Ford, ed. (Ames: Iowa State University Press), pp. 3–16.

166   *References*

Foucault, Michael, 1972. *The Discourse on Language* (New York: Random House).

Franklin, John Hope, 1967. *From Slavery to Freedom* (New York: Vintage Books).

Frazier, E. Franklin, 1963. *The Negro Church in America* (New York: Schocken).

———, 1966. *The Negro in the United States* (New York: Macmillan).

Friedman, John, and John Miller, 1965. The Urban Field. *Journal of the American Institute of Planners* 3:312–20.

Friedman, Samuel R., et al., 1987. The AIDS Epidemic Among Blacks and Hispanics. *Milbank Quarterly* 65 (supplement 2):455–99.

Garrison, Janis R., 1985. Oral history, interviewed by Alan Cherry, 10 May, LDS Afro-American, Brigham Young University.

Gastil, Raymond D., 1975. *Cultural Regions of the United States* (Seattle: University of Washington Press).

Geertz, C., 1962. The Rotating Credit Association: A Middle Rung in Development. *Economic Development and Cultural Change*, 10(3):241–63.

———, 1973. *The Interpretation of Culture* (New York: Basic Books).

Genovese, Eugene, 1974. *Roll Jordan, Roll: The World the Slaves Made* (New York: Vintage Books).

Georgia Department of Human Resources, 1987. *Georgia Disease Patterns of the 80's with Epidemiological Profiles.* Division of Public Health, Georgia Center for Health Statistics (January).

Gewin, V., 1906. Careless and Unscientific Midwifery with Special Reference to Some Features of the Work of Midwives. *Alabama Medical Journal* 18:629–35.

Gibbs, T. K., K. Cagill, L. S. Lieberman, and E. Reitze, 1980. Nutrition in a Slave Population: An Anthropological Examination. *Medical Anthropology* 4:175–262.

Gilkes, Cheryl Townsend, 1990. Together and In Happiness: Women's Tradition in the Sanctified Church. In *Black Women in America,* Micheline R. Malson, ed. (Chicago: University of Chicago Press), pp. 223–44.

Goldsmith, Peter D., 1989. *When I Rise Cryin' Holy: African American Denominationalism on the Georgia Coast* (New York: AMS Press).

Good, Byron J., 1977. The Health of What's the Matter: The Semantics of Illness in Iran. *Culture, Medicine and Psychiatry* 1:25–58.

Gordiner, Nadine, 1989. The Gap Between the Writer and the Reader. *New York Review of Books,* 28 Sept., pp. 59–61.

Gray, L., 1976. A Mental Health Research Agenda for the Black Community. *Journal of Afro-American Issues* 4:278–82.

Gwaltney, John, 1980. *Drylongso: A Self Portrait of Black America* (New York: Random House).

Hall, Bob, 1990. "The Green Scorecard": Ranking the South's Environment. *Southern Exposure* 28(1):49–52.

Hamilton, Green P., 1910. *Bright Side of Memphis* (Memphis, Tenn.: G. P. Hamilton).

Hannerz, Ulf, 1970. What Ghetto Males Are Like: Another Look. In *Afro-American Anthropology: Contemporary Perspectives,* Norman Whitten, Jr., and John Szwed, eds. (New York: Free Press), pp. 313–25.

Hansen, Klaus J., 1981. *Mormonism and the American Experience* (Chicago: University of Chicago Press).

Hardin, E. R., 1924. Midwives. *North Carolina State Board of Health Bulletin* 39:21–24.

———, 1925. The Midwife Problem. *Southern Medical Journal* 18:347–50.

Hare, Nathan, and Julian Hare, 1970. Black Women. *Transaction* 8:65–68.

Harkins, John E., 1982. *Metropolis of the American Nile* (Woodland Hills, Calif.: Windson).

Harris, Gehrig L., 1988. Oral history, interviewed by Alan Cherry, 10 June 1987, LDS Afro-American, Brigham Young University.

Harris, Marvin, 1985. *Good to Eat, Riddles of Food and Culture* (New York: Simon and Schuster).

Harrison, Ira, 1966. The Storefront Church as a Revitalization Movement. *Review of Religious Research* 7:160–63.

Harrison, Ira E., and Diana S. Harrison, 1971. The Black Family Experience and Health Behavior. In *Health and the Family,* Charles O. Crawford, ed. (New York: Macmillan), pp. 175–99.

Herskovits, Melville, 1941. *The Myth of the Negro Past* (New York: Harper and Brothers).

Hill, Carole E., 1988. *Community Health Systems in the Rural American South: Linking People and Policy* (Boulder, Colo.: Westview Press).

Hilliard, Sam B., 1972. *Hog Meat and Hoecake: Food Supply in the Old South* (Carbondale: Southern Illinois University Press).

Hilts, Philip, 1989. Growing Gap in Life Expectancies of Blacks and Whites Is Emerging. *New York Times,* 9 Oct., Sec. I, p 8.

Hine, Ed, 1987. Rx for the Medically Indigent: State Should Step in to Aid 'Working Poor' Denied Medicare, Medicaid. *Atlanta Journal and Constitution,* 26 Apr.

Hobbs, S. H., Jr., 1927. Births Attended by Midwives. *North Carolina State Board of Health Bulletin* 42:26–29.

Hollenweger, Walter J., 1974. *Pentecost Between Black and White: Five Case Studies on Pentecost and Politics* (Belfast: Christian Journals).

168   *References*

Holt, J. B., 1940. Holiness Religion: Cultural Shock and Social Reorganization. *American Sociological Review* 5:740–47.

Hopkins, Donald R., 1987. AIDS in Minority Populations in the United States. *Public Health Reports* 102(6):677–81.

Hudson, Winthrop, 1973. *Religion in America: An Historical Account of the Development of American Religious Life* (New York: Charles Scribner's Sons).

Hurston, Zora Neale, 1935. *Of Mules and Men* (Philadelphia: Lippincott).

———, 1981. *The Sanctified Church* (Berkeley, Calif.: Turtle Island).

Hutton, C. W., and R. B. Hayes-Davis, 1983. Assessment of the Zinc Nutritional Status of Selected Elderly Subjects. *Journal of the American Dietetic Association* 82(2):148–53.

Hyman, H. H., and C. R. Wright, 1971. Trends in Voluntary Association Memberships of American Adults: Replication Based on Secondary Analysis of National Sample Surveys. *American Sociological Review* 36:191–206.

Jackson, Jacquelyne Johnson, 1981. Urban Black Americans. In *Ethnicity and Medical Care,* Alan Harwood, ed. (Cambridge: Harvard University Press), pp. 37–129.

Jacobson, Cardell K., 1989. Black Mormons in the 1980s: Pioneers in a White Church (paper presented at meetings of the Society for the Scientific Study of Religion and Religious Research Association).

Jacquet, Constant H., Jr., ed., 1985. *Yearbook of American and Canadian Churches* (Nashville: Abingdon).

Jerome, N. W., R. F. Kandel, and G. H. Pelto, eds., 1980a. *Nutritional Anthropology: Contemporary Approaches to Diet and Culture* (Pleasantville, N.Y.: Redgrave Press).

Jerome, N. W., G. H. Pelto, and R. F. Kandel, 1980b. An Ecological Approach to Nutritional Anthropology. In *Nutritional Anthropology: Contemporary Approaches to Diet and Culture,* N. W. Jerome, R. T. Kandel, and G. H. Pelto, eds. (Pleasantville, N.Y.: Redgrave Press), pp. 13–46.

Johnson, Daniel, and Rex Campbell, 1981. *Black Migration in America* (Durham, N.C.: Duke University Press).

Johnson, O., 1966. *The History of the Yorubas* (London: Routledge & Kegan Paul).

Jones, James H., 1981. *Bad Blood: The Tuskegee Syphilis Experiment* (New York: Free Press).

Jones, Le Roi [Imamu Baraka], 1963. *Blues People: Negro Music in White America* (Westport, Conn.: Greenwood Press).

Jones, Raymond, 1939. A Comparative Study of Religious Cult Behavior Among Negroes with Special Reference to Emotional Conditioning Factors. *Howard University Studies in the Social Sciences* 2:100–104.

Jones, Woodrow, Jr., and Mitchell F. Rice, 1987. Black Health Care: An

Overview. In *Health Care Issues in Black America: Policies, Problems, and Prospects,* Woodrow Jones, Jr., and Mitchell F. Rice, eds. (New York: Greenwood Press), pp. 3–20.

Joyner, Charles, 1972. Soul Food and the Sambo Stereotype: Folklore from the Slave Narrative Collection. *Keystone Folklore Quarterly* (Winter):171–78.

Kerri, James N., 1976. Studying Voluntary Associations as Adaptive Mechanisms: A Review of Anthropological Perspectives. *Current Anthropology* 17:25–36.

Kimball, Solon, and Marion B. Pearsall, 1954. *The Talladega Story: A Study in Community Process* (Tuscaloosa: University of Alabama Press).

Klobus-Edwards, P., J. N. Edwards, and D. L. Klemmack, 1978. Difference in Social Participation: Blacks and Whites. *Social Forces* 56:1035–54.

Kobrin, Frances E., 1966. The American Midwife Controversy: A Crisis of Professionalization. *Bulletin of the History of Medicine* 15:350–63.

Korn, Bertram, 1961. Jews and Negro Slavery in the Old South 1789–1865. *Publications of the American Jewish Historical Society* 1:151–201.

Kornweibel, Theodore, 1981. *In Search of the Promised Land* (Port Washington, N.Y.: Kennikat Press).

Kroll-Smith, J. Stephen, 1980. The Testimony as Performance: The Relationship of an Expressive Event to the Belief System. *Journal for the Scientific Study of Religion* 19:16–25.

Kunkel, Peter, and Sara Sue Kennard, 1971. *Spout Spring: A Black Community* (New York: Holt, Rinehart and Winston).

Ladner, Joyce A., 1972. *Tomorrow's Tomorrow: The Black Woman* (Garden City, N.Y.: Doubleday).

Lamb, Anne, and Rebecca Swindell, 1954. Training and Supervision of Midwives in North Carolina. *North Carolina State Board of Health Bulletin* 69:7–14.

Landes, Ruth, 1967. Negro Jews in Harlem. *Jewish Journal of Sociology* 9:175–89.

Landing, James, 1974. The Spatial Expression of Cultural Revitalization in Chicago. *Proceedings of the Association of American Geographers* 6:50–53.

Landry, Bart, 1987. *The New Black Middle Class* (Berkeley: University of California Press).

Lane, Brenda, 1989. You Can Go Home Again. *American Visions,* April, pp. 24–27.

LDS Afro-American Symposium, 1988. Provo, Utah: Brigham Young University, 8 June. Videotape.

Leonardo, Micaela di, 1991. Women's Culture and Its Discontents. In *The Politics of Culture,* Brett Williams, ed. (Washington, D.C.: Smithsonian Institution Press), pp. 219–42.

Levine, Lawrence, 1977. *Black Culture and Black Consciousness: Afro-American Folk Thought from Slavery to Freedom* (New York: Oxford University Press).

Lewis, Diane K., 1990. A Response to Inequality: Black Women, Racism, and Sexism. In *Black Women in America,* Micheline R. Malson, et al. (Chicago: University of Chicago Press), pp. 41–63.

Liebow, Elliot, 1967. *Tally's Corner* (Boston: Little, Brown and Company).

Litoff, Judy Barrett, 1978. *America Midwives: 1860 to the Present* (Westport, Conn.: Greenwood Press).

———, 1986. *The American Midwife Debate* (Westport, Conn.: Greenwood).

Little, Kenneth, 1966. *West African Urbanization: A Study of Voluntary Associations in Social Change* (London: Cambridge University Press).

Lougee, George, 1964. Midwife—A Special Breed of Angel. *The Durham Morning Herald* (Durham, N.C.), 27 Apr., Sec. B, p. 2.

MacGregor, Rob Roy, 1987. Alcohol and Drugs as Co-Factors for AIDS. *AIDS and Substance Abuse* 7(2):47–71.

MacRobert, Iain, 1988. *The Black Roots and White Racism of Early Pentecostalism in the USA* (New York: St. Martin's Press).

Malinowski, Bronislaw, 1944. *A Scientific Theory of Culture and Other Essays* (Chapel Hill: University of North Carolina Press).

Marable, Manning, 1981. *Blackwater: Historical Studies in Race, Class Consciousness and Revolution* (Dayton: Black Praxis Press).

———, 1984. *Race, Reform and Rebellion: The Second Reconstruction in Black America, 1945–1982* (Jackson: University Press of Mississippi).

———, 1990. Black Politics and the Challenges for the Left. *Monthly Review* 41(11):22–31.

Marks, Carole, 1981. Split Labor Markets and Black-White Relations, 1865–1920. *Phylon* 2:293–308.

Marshall, Ray, 1977. Black Employment in the South. In *Women, Minorities, and Employment Discrimination,* Phyllis A. Wallace and Annett M. Lamond, eds. (Lexington, Mass.: D. C. Heath and Company), pp. 57–81.

Mauss, Armand L., 1981. The Fading of Pharoah's Curse: The Decline and Fall of the Priesthood Ban Against Blacks in the Mormon Church. *Dialogue* 14(3):10–45.

McKinney, John C., and Linda Barogue, 1971. The Changing South: National Incorporation of a Region. *American Sociological Review* 36(3):399–412.

McMillen, Neil, 1989. *Dark Journey: Black Mississippians in the Age of Jim Crow* (Urbana: University of Illinois Press).

McMurray, Georgia L., 1990. Those of Broader Vision: An African-American Perspective on Teenage Pregnancy and Parenting. In *The Status of Black America,* Janet Dewart, ed. (New York: National Urban League).

McNeill, William Hardy, 1976. *Plaques and Peoples* (Garden City, N.Y.: Anchor Press).

Meier, August, 1963. *Negro Thought in America, 1880–1915* (Ann Arbor: University of Michigan Press).

Meier, August, and Elliot Rudwick, 1970. *From Plantation to Ghetto* (New York: Hill and Wang).

Melton, J. Gordon, 1978. *The Encyclopedia of American Religions*, vol. I. (Wilmington, N.D.: McGrath).

Mintz, Sidney W., 1977. The So-Called World System: Local Initiative and Local Response. *Dialectical Anthropology* 2:253–70.

Molgaad, Graig, et al., 1988. Assessing Alcoholism as a Risk Factor For Acquired Immunodeficiency Syndrome (AIDS). *Social Science and Medicine* 27N:1147–52.

Mongeau, Beatrice, Harvey L. Smith, and Ann C. Maney, 1961. The "Granny" Midwife: Changing Roles and Functions of a Folk Practitioner. *American Journal of Sociology* 66:497–501.

Morris, Aldon D., 1984. *The Origins of the Civil Rights Movement: Black Communities Organizing for Change* (New York: Free Press).

Myers, Katherine, 1921. The Midwife: A Factor in Infant and Maternal Health. *North Carolina State Board of Health Bulletin* 36:1–9.

Myrdal, Gunnar, Richard Sterner, and Arnold Rose, 1944. *An American Dilemma: The Negro Problem and Modern Democracy* (New York: Harper).

National Center for Health Statistics, 1982. *Blood Pressure Levels and Hypertension in Persons Aged 6–74 Years: United States, 1976–80.* In Advance Data for Vital and Health Statistics, no. 84, DHHS Pub. no. (PHS) 82-1250.

National Urban League, 1983. *The State of Black America, 1983* (New York: National Urban League.)

National Women's Health Report, 1990. Health Care in the U.S.: The Gaps are Widening. *National Women's Health Report* 12:6.

Neal, William F., 1985. *Southern Cooking* (Chapel Hill: University of North Carolina Press).

Nelson, H. M., R. A. Yokley, and A. K. Nelson, eds., 1971. *The Black Church in America* (New York: Basic Books).

Nelsen, Hart, and Anne Nelsen, 1975. *Black Church in the Sixties* (Lexington: University of Kentucky Press).

North Carolina, 1971. *Report of the Committee on the Physician Shortage in Rural North Carolina to the Legislative Research Commission of the North Carolina General Assembly.* General Assembly of North Carolina. Raleigh, N.C.

———, 1977. General Statutes. Raleigh, N.C.

———, 1981a. Journal of the House of Representatives of the General Assembly of the State of North Carolina. First Session, Raleigh, N.C.

———, 1981b. State of North Carolina Session Laws and Resolutions Passed by the 1981 General Assembly, Raleigh, N.C.

———, 1983a. Journal of the Senate of the General Assembly of the State of North Carolina, First Session, Raleigh, N.C.

———, 1983b. Journal of the House of Representatives of the General Assembly of the State of North Carolina. First Session, Raleigh, N.C.

———, 1988. *North Carolina Vital Statistics,* vol. 1. Raleigh: North Carolina Department of Environment, Health, and Natural Resources, Division of Statistics and Information Services.

———, 1989. *North Carolina Vital Statistics,* vol. 1. Raleigh: North Carolina Department of Environment, Health, and Natural Resources, Division of Statistics and Information Services.

North Carolina State Board of Health, 1917. Controlling the Midwife Problem. *Bulletin* 32:108–9.

———, 1925. Importance of Midwife Control: Proposed Plan of Instruction Outlined. *Bulletin* 40:5–9.

———, 1927. Midwife and Mortality Statistics. *Bulletin* 42:29–31.

———, 1932, Midwife Control. *Bulletin* 47:3–5.

———, 1936. Notes on Maternal Mortality. *Bulletin* 51:12.

Noyes, C., 1912. Training of Midwives in Relation to the Prevention of Infant Mortality. *American Journal of Obstetrics* 66:1051–59.

Ortner, Sherry, 1984. Theory in Anthropology Since the Sixties. *Comparative Studies in Society and History* 26:126–66.

Parker, Robert, 1937. *The Incredible Messiah* (Boston: Little, Brown and Co.).

Patterson, James Oglethorpe, 1984. *"The Mother Church"* (Memphis, Tenn.: Pentecostal Temple Institutional Church of God in Christ).

Pressman, Sonia, 1970. Job Discrimination and the Black Woman. *Crises* 3:103–8.

Powdermaker, Hortense, 1939. *After Freedom: A Cultural Study in the Deep South* (New York: Atheneum).

Proctor, Ivan, 1923. A Plea for Better Obstetrics in the State of North Carolina. *Transactions of the Medical Society of North Carolina* 70:115–20.

Puckett, Newbell N., 1926. *Folk Beliefs of the Southern Negro* (Chapel Hill: University of North Carolina Press).

Pulley, Elizabeth. 1985. Oral history, interviewed by Alan Cherry, 19 Oct., LDS Afro-American, Brigham Young University.

Queen, Jacqueline B., 1982. 1981 North Carolina Health Legislation. *Health Law Bulletin* 57:1–17.

Raboteau, Albert, 1978. *Slave Religion* (Oxford: Oxford University Press).

Radcliffe-Brown, A. R., 1965. *Structure and Function in Primitive Society:*

Essays and Addresses (New York: Free Press).

Radin, Charles, 1990. Academics' Role Smaller than Abroad. *Boston Globe*, 1 Mar.

Rainwater, Lee, 1970. *Behind Ghetto Walls* (Chicago: Aldine).

Rankin, W. S., 1925. Annual Report, North Carolina State Board of Health. *North Carolina State Board of Health Bulletin* 40:13–14.

Raper, Arthur, 1926. *Preface to Peasantry* (Chapel Hill: University of North Carolina Press).

Redkey, Edwin, 1969. *Black Exodus* (New Haven: Yale University Press).

Reed, Adolph, 1986. *The Jesse Jackson Phenomenon* (New Haven: Yale University Press).

――――, 1988. The Liberal Technocrat. *The Nation*, 6 Feb., pp. 167–170.

Reid, Ira, 1926. Let Us Prey. *Opportunity* 4:274–78.

――――, 1940. *In A Minor Key* (Washington, D.C.: American Council on Education).

Reid, Rosalind, 1980. Repeal of Midwifery Law Urged. *News and Observer* (Raleigh, N.C.), 8 March, Sec. A, p. 7.

Rene, Antonio A., 1987. Racial Differences in Mortality: Blacks and Whites. In *Health Care Issues in Black America: Policies, Problems, and Prospects*, Woodrow Jones, Jr., and Mitchell F. Rice, eds. (Westport, Conn.: Greenwood Press).

Robinson, Robert, n.d. *An Introduction to Church of God in Christ: History, Theology and Structure* (Little Rock, Ark.: Robert Robinson).

Rothenberg, Paula S., 1988. *Racism and Sexism: An Integrated Study* (New York: St. Martin's Press).

Rubin, Morton, 1951. *Plantation County* (Chapel Hill: University of North Carolina Press).

Sacks, Karen, 1988. *Caring by the Hour* (Urbana: University of Illinois Press).

Sahlins, Marshall, 1976. *Culture and Practical Reason* (Chicago: University of Chicago Press).

Sanders, Charles L., 1980. Some Critical Issues and Problems of Black Managers in Black Organizations. In *Black Organizations: Issues on Survival Techniques*, Lennox S. Yearwood, ed. (Washington, D.C.: University Press of America), pp. 179–92.

Sangster, Ian, 1973. *Sugar and Jamaica* (London: Thomas Nelson and Sons).

Savitt, Todd L., 1978. *Medicine and Slavery: The Disease and Health Care of Blacks in Antebellum Virginia* (Urbana: University of Illinois Press).

――――, 1984. The Education of Black Physicians at Shaw University, 1882–1918. In *Black Americans in North Carolina and the South*, Jeffrey J. Crow and Flora J. Hatley, eds. (Chapel Hill: University of North Carolina Press), pp. 160–88.

————, 1988. Slave Health and Southern Distinctiveness. In *Disease and Distinctiveness in the American South,* Todd L. Savitt and James Harvey Young, eds. (Knoxville: University of Tennessee Press).

Schulz, David A., 1969. *Coming Up Black: Patterns of Ghetto Socialization* (Englewood Cliffs, N.J.: Prentice-Hall).

Seals, A. M., and J. Kolaja, 1964. Study of Negro Voluntary Organizations in Lexington, Kentucky. *Phylon* 25:27–32.

Shapiro, Deanne, 1970. *Double Damnation, Double Salvation: The Sources and Varieties of Black Judaism in the United States* (M.A. thesis, Columbia University).

————, 1974. Factors in the Development of Black Judaism. In *The Black Experience in Religion,* C. Eric Lincoln, ed. (Garden City, N.Y.: Doubleday), pp. 254–72.

Sheppardson, George, and Thomas Price, 1958. *The Independent African* (Edinburgh: Edinburgh University Press).

Shimkin, E., D. Shimkin, and D. Frante, 1978. *The Extended Family in Black Societies* (The Hague: Mouton).

Shopshire, James Maynard, 1975. A Socio-Historical Characterization of the Black Pentecostal Movement in America (Ph.D. diss., Northwestern University).

Sigerist, Henry E., 1943. *Civilization and Disease* (Ithaca, N.Y.: Cornell University Press).

Silverman, Marilyn, 1979. Dependency, Mediation, and Class Formation in Rural Guyana. *American Ethnologist* 6:466–90.

Simey, Thomas S., 1946. *Welfare and Planning in the West Indies* (Oxford: Clarendon Press).

Simpson, George Eaton, 1978. *Black Religions in the New World* (New York: Columbia University Press).

Singer, Merrill, 1979. Saints of the Kingdom: Group Emergence, Individual Affiliation, and Social Change Among the Black Hebrews of Israel (Ph.D. diss., University of Utah).

————, 1982. Life in a Defensive Society: The Black Hebrew Israelites. In *Sex Roles in Contemporary American Communes,* Jon Wagner, ed. (Bloomington: Indiana University Press), pp. 45–81.

————, 1985. "Now I Know What the Songs Mean!": Traditional Black Music in a Contemporary Black Sect. *Southern Quarterly* 23:125–40.

Smiley, Cleeretta H., 1988. Oral history, interview by Alan Cherry, 10 Oct. 1986, LDS Afro-American, Brigham Young University.

Smith, H. Shelton, 1972. *In His Image But . . . : Racism in Southern Religion* (Durham, N.C.: Duke University Press).

Smith, Joseph, Jr., 1978. *History of the Church of Jesus Christ of Latter-day Saints, Period I,* vol. I, rev. ed. (Salt Lake City: Desert Books).

Solberg, Patrice, 1979. 1979 Health Legislation. *Health Law Bulletin* 53:1–14.

Spear, Allan, 1967. *Black Chicago: The Making of a Negro Ghetto, 1890–1920* (Chicago: University of Chicago Press).

Spencer, Boris, 1985. Oral history, interviewed by Alan Cherry, 17 May, LDS Afro-American, Brigham Young University.

Stack, Carol B., 1974. *All Our Kin: Strategies for Survival in a Black Community* (New York: Harper and Row).

Stall, Ron, 1987. The Prevention of HIV Infection Associated with Drug and Alcohol Use During Sexual Activity. *Aids and Substance* 7(2):73–89.

Staples, Robert, 1973. *The Black Woman in America: Sex, Marriage, and the Family* (Chicago: Nelson Hall).

Susie, Debra Anne, 1988. *In the Way of Our Grandmothers* (Athens: University of Georgia Press).

Synan, Vinson, 1971. *The Holiness-Pentecostal Movement in the States* (Grand Rapids, Mich.: W. B. Eerdmans).

———, 1986. The Quiet Rise of Black Pentecostals. *Charisma* 11(11):45–49, 55.

Taussig, F., 1917. The Nurse-Midwife. *Wisconsin Medical Journal* 15:113–15.

Taylor, Joe G., 1982. *Eating, Drinking and Visiting in the South: An Informal History* (Baton Rouge: Louisiana State University Press).

Thomas, Charles E., 1986. *Jelly-Roll: A Black Neighborhood in a Southern Mill Town* (Little Rock, Ark.: Rose).

Tindall, George B., 1974. Beyond the Mainstream: The Ethnic Southern. *Journal of Southern History* 40:3–18.

Tinney, James S., 1978. A Theoretical and Historical Comparison of Black Political and Religious Movements (Ph.D. diss., Howard University).

Todhunter, E. N., 1976. Lifestyle and Nutrient Intake in the Elderly. *Current Concepts in Nutrition* 4:119–27.

Trouillot, Michael-Ralph, 1984. Caribbean Pleasantries and World Capitalism: An Approach to Micro-Level Studies: *Nieuwe West-Indische Gids* 58:37–59.

Tucker, David M., 1975. *Black Pastors and Leaders: Memphis 1819–1972* (Memphis, Tenn.: Memphis State University Press).

Turner, Burl, Jr., 1989. Oral history, interviewed by Alan Cherry, 11 June 1987, LDS Afro-American, Brigham Young University.

Underwood, F., 1926. Development of Midwifery in Mississippi. *Southern Medical Journal* 19:683–85.

United States, 1932. *White House Conference on Child Health and Protection, Midwives* (New York: D. Appleton-Century).

United States Department of Health and Human Services, 1985. *Health Status of Minorities and Low Income Groups.* DHHS Publication No. HRS-P-DV 85-1 (Washington, D.C.: Government Printing Office).

————, 1989. *Report of the Secretary's Task Force on Black and Minority Health,* vol. 6, Infant Mortality and Low Birthweight (Washington, D.C.: Government Printing Office).

Uya, Okon Edet, 1971. Life in the Slave Community. *Afro-American Studies* 1:281–90.

Vaughan, Kate Brew, 1919. The Aims of the Bureau of Infant Hygiene to Be Accomplished Through County Nurses. *North Carolina State Board of Health Bulletin* 34(8):13–14.

Vogel, Morris J., 1980. *The Invention of the Modern Hospital: Boston, 1870–1930* (Chicago: University of Chicago Press).

Vontress, Clement, 1971. The Black Male Personality. *Black Scholar* 2:10–17.

Wall, R. L., Jr., 1956. Three Centuries of Obstetrics in North Carolina. *North Carolina Medical Journal* 17:355–67.

Walker, Lynn, 1973. On Employment Discrimination. *Essence* 4:24.

Walter, Eugene, 1971. *American Cooking: Southern Style* (New York: Time-Life).

Warner, W. Lloyd, and Allison Davis, 1939. A Comparative Study of American Caste. In *Race Relations and the Race Problem,* Edgar Thomas, ed. (Durham, N.C.: Duke University Press).

Warren, David C., 1972. Legitimization of Nurse-Midwives. *Health Law Bulletin* 33:1–4.

————, 1974. The Legal Basis for the Training and Utilization of Nurse-Midwives. *Health Law Bulletin* 43:1–4.

Washington, Booker T., 1902. *The Future of the American Negro* (Boston: Small, Maynard and Company).

Wayne, Leslie, 1971. Are "Granny Midwives" on the Way Out Here? *News and Observer* (Raleigh, N.C.), 1 Aug., Sec. B, p. 3.

Webb, Craig, 1981. Ban on Midwives Opposed by Panel. *News and Observer* (Raleigh, N.C.), 25 May, p. 14.

What If . . . ? School of Medicine Has Contributed, 1990. *Daily Reflector* (Greenville, N.C.), 3 Apr., Sec. A, p. 4.

White, O. Kendall, Jr., 1972. Mormonism's Anti-Black Policy and Prospects for Change. *Journal of Religious Thought* 29(2):38–60.

————, 1981/1982. Boundary Maintenance, Blacks, and the Mormon Priesthood. *Journal of Religious Thought* 37(2):30–44.

————, 1986. Ideology of the Family in Nineteenth Century Mormonism. *Sociological Spectrum* 6:289–305.

————, 1989. Mormonism and the Equal Rights Amendment. *Journal of Church and State* 31:249–67.

White, O. Kendall, Jr., and Daryl White, 1980. Abandoning an Unpopular Policy: An Analysis of the Decision Granting the Mormon Priesthood to Blacks. *Sociological Analysis* 41:231–45.

Whitehead, Tony L., 1984. Sociocultural Dynamics and Food Habits in a Southern Community. In *Food in the Social Order: Studies of Food and Festivities in Three American Communities,* Mary Douglas, ed. (New York: Russell Sage Foundation).

————, 1989. *The Black Family: The Encyclopedia of Southern Culture* (Chapel Hill: University of North Carolina Press).

Whitehead, T. L., and E. J. Wright, 1987. Socio-Cultural Aspects of Obesity in a North Carolina Community. *Social Science* 72(1):38–43.

Wiley, Bell Irwin, 1938. *Southern Negroes: 1861–1865* (New Haven: Yale University Press).

Williams, Charles, 1982. Black Religion and the Black Church: A Southern Experience (unpublished manuscript).

Williams, Charles, and Hilda Booker Williams, 1984. Contemporary Voluntary Associations in the Urban Black Church: The Development and Growth of Mutual Aid Societies. *Journal of Voluntary Action Research* 13(4):19–30.

Williams, J. Whitridge, 1912. Medical Education and the Midwife Problem in the United States. *Journal of the American Medical Association* 58:1–7.

Williams, Melvin, 1974. *Community in a Black Pentecostal Church: An Anthropological Study* (Pittsburgh: University of Pittsburgh Press).

Wilmore, Gayraud, 1972. *Black Religion and Black Radicalism* (Garden City, N.Y.: Anchor Press).

————, 1983. *Black Religion and Black Radicalism,* rev. ed. (Maryknoll, N.Y.: Orbis).

Wilson, Bryan R., 1969. A Typology of Sects. In *Sociology of Religion: Readings,* Roland Robertson, ed. (Baltimore: Penguin), pp. 361–83.

Wilson, William J., 1987. *The Truly Disadvantaged: The Inner City, the Underclass, and Public Policy* (Chicago: University of Chicago Press).

Wolf, Eric, 1982. *Europe and the People Without History* (Berkeley: University of California Press).

Woodson, Carter G., 1945. *The History of the Negro Church* (Washington, D.C.: Associated Press).

Wong, Bernard P., 1982. *Chinatown: Economic Adaptation and Ethnic Identity of the Chinese* (New York: Holt, Rinehart and Winston).

Wright, E. J., 1986. Sociocultural Aspects of Body Image: Explorations of Body Size and Weight Problem Perceptions in a Southern Community (Ph.D. diss., University of North Carolina, Chapel Hill).

Wright, E. J., and T. L. Whitehead, 1987. Perceptions of Body Size and Obesity: A Selected Review of the Literature. *Journal of Community Health*

12(2/3):117–29.

Wright, Van C., Sr., 1989. Oral history, interviewed by Alan Cherry, 10 June 1987, LDS Afro-American, Brigham Young University.

Ziegler, C., 1913. The Elimination of the Midwife. *Journal of the American Medical Association* 55:32–38.

Contributors

HANS A. BAER is professor in the Department of Sociology and Anthropology at the University of Arkansas at Little Rock. He has conducted research on the Hutterites in South Dakota, the Levites of Utah, African American religion and ethnomedicine, osteopathy, chiropractic, and naturopathy in the United States and Britain, and social life in the German Democratic Republic. He is the author of *The Black Spiritual Movement: A Religious Response to Racism* and *Recreating Utopia in the Desert: A Sectarian Response to Modern Mormonism* and is the editor of *Encounters with Biomedicine: Case Studies in Medical Anthropology*.

ANNIE S. BARNES is professor in the Department of Sociology at Norfolk State University in Norfolk, Virginia. She is the author of *Single Parents in Black America* and *Black Women: Interpersonal Relationships in Profile*. She served as the president of the Association of Black American Anthropologists during 1990–91.

JOHNNETTA COLE is the first African American woman to serve as president of Spelman College. She formerly was professor of Anthropology and director of the Latin American and Caribbean Studies Program at Hunter College of the City University of New York. She edited *All American Women: Lines That Divide, Ties That Bind* and *Anthropology for the Nineties: Introductory Readings*.

IRA E. HARRISON is associate professor in the Department of Anthropology at the University of Tennessee in Knoxville. His research interests are African American anthropology, traditional medicine, public health, urban anthropology, and Africa.

CAROLE E. HILL is professor of Anthropology at Georgia State University in Atlanta. She has conducted extensive research on health-related issues in Costa Rica and in various populations in the American South, including African Americans. She authored *Community Health Systems in the Rural South: Linking People and Policy* and edited *Current Health Policy Issues and Alternatives: An Applied Social Science Perspective*.

YVONNE JONES is associate professor of Anthropology and chairperson of the Department of Pan-African Studies at the University of Louisville. She has conducted extensive research on African American enterpreneurial activities.

HOLLY F. MATHEWS is associate professor of Anthropology at East Carolina University. She has applied her interest in cognitive anthropology to the study of aging and rural health problems as well as to comparative analyses of issues of gender, race, and class in Latin America and the Southern United States. She edited *Women in the South: An Anthropological Perspective*.

MERRILL SINGER is director of research at the Hispanic Health Council in Hartford, Connecticut. He has conducted field and survey research with several ethnic and religious communities in Los Angeles, Salt Lake City, Washington, D.C., Miami, Israel, and Haiti. He has published extensively on topics of religious conversion, religious movements, health behavior, medical anthropology theory, and the political economy of health. In recent years, his research and applied work has focused especially on the issues of substance abuse and AIDS in African American and Hispanic communities.

DARYL WHITE teaches anthropology and sociology at Spelman College in Atlanta, Georgia. Most of his research has focused on southern Protestantism and Mormonism. With his brother, Kendall, he is currently writing a book about Mormon racism.

O. KENDALL WHITE is professor of Sociology and chair of the Department of Sociology and Anthropology at Washington and Lee University in Lexington, Virginia. His research and writing have concentrated primarily on anthropological and sociological aspects of religion, particularly Mormonism.

TONY L. WHITEHEAD is chairperson of the Department of Anthropology at the University of Maryland, College Park. As director of the department's Cultural Systems Analysis Group, he directs research on AIDS, drug trafficking, and health and food behavior. He formerly taught in the School of Public Health at the University of North Carolina at Chapel Hill.

BRETT WILLIAMS is associate professor in the Department of Anthropology at American University in Washington, D.C. She edited *The Politics of Culture*.

CHARLES WILLIAMS, JR., is associate professor in the Department of Anthropology at Memphis State University. His main research interests are community health, alcoholism, religion, and mutual aid societies. Dr. Williams has done field research on African Americans in Mississippi and Tennessee.

HILDA J. B. WILLIAMS has research interests in self-help activities, including mutual aid societies. She currently is training coordinator for the Physical Plant and Planning Department at Memphis State University.